White Christian Domination: When will it End

Their Initiation of all World Conflicts and the end results

RAY HOUSE

White Christian domination when will it end

Copyright © 2013 Ray House

ISBN: 061580083
ISBN-13: 978-0615800486

Dedication

I give my dedication to God the Creator of the heavens and the earth and May peace and blessings be on Prophet Muhammad, who came as a mercy to mankind, who spoke guidance and wisdom, and on his forefather Ibrahim, and brothers, Moses and Jesus and all the Prophets. I thank God for still being on this earth with my sanity able to write this book, have mercy on me and accept me in His heaven and most important protect me from evil perpetrators. And all Praise be to GOD, Lord of the worlds. Ameen.

Acknowledgments
Wife: Merieme,
Children: Sarah, Mahmoud
Cleopatra and Tamika

Contents

Reference charts of facts and evidence

Preface

This book is written from the perspective of the persecuting people, the underdogs, the non-conquers, the indigenous ones, the enslaved, the colonized, and the oppressed all over the global world. The end results of most history were wars written from the victor's point of view even though they may be the perpetrators, the aggressive invaders, the ones with superior weapons, and the cause of the war, therefore, their pen may lie, and give them glory.

The combination of world history and religion presents one with enjoyable reading, but whose perspective is the most prevalent? Reading the history of the British Empire from the European perspective suggests that historically, they did nothing wrong. According to Eurocentric writers, every country that was influenced by the British was "blessed." They do not talk about the British slave trade, the invasion of Africa and Asia, or the various global massacres that the British initiated.

Reading this book will also provide those interested in religious historical literature, with an understanding of the histories of the Ibrahimic faiths (Judaism, Christianity, and Islam) and the Medieval Era when the sailing Crusaders and Knights launched wars against the Muslims in the Levant. Over the following 300 years, organized European Christians depopulated indigenous cultures all over the world by enforcing acculturation and assimilation through the enslavement and colonization of the greater part of Africa and Southeast Asia.

I wrote this book because people need a different perspective of world history, world religions, and world secularism. The people in the West are told that they have freedoms, but in reality, they are controlled, dominated, and psychologically brainwashed. This book is written in chronological order based on major historical events. Children in school receive an extremely diluted version of world history. All of Native American history has been erased and only one paragraph on slavery and Jim Crow history are taught. Therefore, I have tried my best to enlighten my audience about the history of the United States, Africa, Asia, Europe, and Australia. I have explained the history of Jesus Christ and how white Christian Europeans devised the trinity doctrine. Unfortunately, the average person's understanding of history is derived from a two-hour Hollywood movie.

Introduction

We have to start in ancient times before the event of Christianity and write about the children of Israel, the Egyptians, Greeks, and Romans. The ancient times the region is the Middle East, North Africa, and Southern Europe. Many people believe and or practice many types of paganism and or beliefs in many deities all but one group the children of Ibrahim, Isaac, and Ishmael who were the only tribes or people that worshipped the one, God. Let's put the stories of the God of Ibrahim on a level where we can understand all the reasons or parables behind the stories.

The action history of the worlds, the topic of mankind's domination, wars, who conquer who, their politics, their religions, and their race derived from the ancient times of Hannibal, Alexander the Great, the Roman Empire, the Persian Empire, and Egyptian Empire. The brush and aggressiveness of the Ibrahimic faiths first Israelites start in slavery and looking for their promised land, Christianity starts with persecution, goes astray then becomes a dominating persecutory force and lastly, Islam starts with control and domination but ends very weak. These dominating faiths do not have a history of friendship towards each other and each claim they are God's choice to salvation in the little land of Jerusalem; the city of peace where all three faiths have sacred sites.

Where they started wars to dominate each other, lots of resentment and spilled blood in their history.

The renaissance coincided with the rejection of Christianity by the leading intellectuals of Europe combined with their uncritical adoration of ancient Greece and Rome.

Most of southern European and North African history was written, but sub-Saharan Africa had an oral tradition and much of their ancient history was based on folklore. Who are the conquerors? What was their religion? What gave them the motivation, confidence, and arrogance to subdue nations? White Christians from Europe are much to blame for the destruction of civilization, and the colonization of Africa, the Middle East, and Asia. They are also responsible for the Transatlantic Slave Trade and the forcible removal of Native Americans from their land. The British Empire caused millions of casualties during its initial invasions and left behind economic chaos, political unrest, and religious conflict. Slavery eventually ended but was followed by Jim Crow in the USA and apartheid in South Africa. Nature itself has not been exempt from the destructive actions, policies, and ignorant thinking of the white race.

The aims, goals, and objectives of the United Nations who do they represent? Their laid-back actions contradict their true intentions.

The big problem of the world is the 500-year-old secularism which is based on the greed of capitalism, the hatred of religions, and the practice of immorality all contributing to too many of the current problems in the world today. Also, the famine in the world, epidemic diseases in the world, and Africa has a host of political problems, issues, and conflicts. Barack Obama, the first President of color, ran a campaign incorporating the word "change," and received tremendous support from Africa, Asia, and even Europe. However Obama has not changed anything he has the same foreign policy as the five Presidents before him, and in the media, he knows how to avoid the main issues. The world continues to be a white Christian dominating spectrum with no end in sight and things will only get worse.

So many people in the world do not see the big picture, because of the white race; they are the teachers, the respected ones, people of wealth and with unmerciful military powers that have will, and continue to destroy innocence living all over the world. What about the people on the street are they happy with the secularist government, the greed/usury base capitalism economy, worse their three-god paganism Christianity religious beliefs. The people need to know the truths of the world, just because a country has material wealth, political power, and military dominance does not make them worthy. Religions are so illogical, the people may know the truth within their hearts but on the outside, they may not be shining in the eyes of the masses. Next, the ferocious big bully five, "the United States, United Kingdom, France, Russia, and China," the first three are overwhelming guilty of attacking and destroying the black race. Also, they are guilty of attacking and destroying the economic system of communism. Lastly, all five are guilty of attacking and destroying the Muslim world and its civilizations.

The path to peace in the world, it is so ironic that the non-white conquer nations of the world continue to as their white conquerors for assistance notwithstanding the historical initial conflicts. Finally, this is a research book encouraging the readers to continue their research in discovering the truth.

Chapter I

Ancient Times

The first examples of the white race's aggression
and the white race supremacy was the Italians'
the attack on the Carthage people
The second example is Alexander of Macedonia
who led attacks on all of the ancient world
The first of the Ibrahimic faith in Jerusalem and their
stories in the land of Canaan and Egypt

Starting in the ancient Egyptian Empire the Israelites were the only people on the earth who worship one God. Following the trials of these people, we must comprehend the broader picture of what God wants of His creatures. If we go a step back to the land of Canaan with Ibrahim who is considered the founder of the one God faith, we see that Ibrahim worshipped one God. His father worshipped the moon and the sun; he challenged Ibrahim's invisible God and gave him a difficult life. However, the Holy books state that God was on Ibrahim's side or was He? Ibrahim wanted children but they did not come until he was over 85 years old. He wanted land or a nation but he died a nomadic and his children eventually received the land that was promised by God, but it came at a cost. The ancient world was mostly polytheistic and the God of Ibrahim always intended for the world to be monotheistic. Moses and the children of Ibrahim were in Egypt where they had no land, and as slaves, God gave Moses the impossible task of converting Pharaoh and releasing his people from bondage. This is an extraordinary spiritual story but God truly helped Moses and the children of Israel (Ya'qoob) to safely escape Egypt and Pharaoh by crossing the Red Sea. As an example to mankind, Pharaoh drowned.

In the land of Canaan, a new task awaited the Israelites: the Philistines. The Philistines were a people that had land, power and their own polytheistic beliefs. Moses spoke with God on top of Mount Sinai. In this conversation, God gave Moses the law (the Ten Commandments), while the weak in faith Israelites were building and worshipping the golden calf, breaking the first commandment. If God's intention was to use the children of Israel as an example to show the people of the ancient world how to worship Him, He surely chose the wrong people. It is amazing that these people who were enslaved had enough gold in their possession to build an idol. God created laws that He knew would be broken. He also created scenarios for His people to break the laws but provided them with free will to ask for forgiveness. The hearts of the Israelites were still in Egypt; therefore, they all remained in the land of Sinai for forty years, where they wandered throughout the land. These defiant and disobedient people died in the desert until the next generation of the Prophet David came to be.

Once young David defeated the giant Goliath, he became Moses' successor as the leader of the Israelites. After the victory of the battle, the children of Jacob now had a state, a nation and land to claim as their own. But living in a polytheistic world with hostile neighbors, made it difficult to do God's work. God desired to make His creation worship Him only and using these weak in faith people to convert the world was a difficult task. Know that the children of Israel and or the Israelites during the times of Moses and David were not considered Jews.

"And [mention, O Muhammad], when Moses said to his people: 'O my people, remember the favour of Allah upon you when He appointed among you prophets and made you possessors and gave you that which He had not given anyone among the worlds. O my people, enter the Holy Land [i.e., Palestine] which Allah has assigned to you and do not turn back [from fighting in Allah's cause] and [thus] become losers.' They said: 'O Moses, indeed within it is a people of tyrannical strength, and indeed, we will never enter it until they leave it, but if they leave it, then we will enter.' Said two wise men from those who feared [to disobey] upon whom Allah had bestowed favour: 'Enter upon them through the gate, for when you have entered it, you will be predominant. And upon Allah rely, if you should be believers.' They said: 'O Moses, indeed we will not enter it, ever, as long as they are within it; so go, you and your Lord, and fight. Indeed, we are remaining right here.' [Moses]

said: 'My Lord, indeed I do not possess [i.e., control] except myself and my brother, so part us from the defiantly disobedient people.' [Allah] said: 'Then indeed, it is forbidden to them for forty years [in which] they will wander throughout the land. So do not grieve over the defiantly disobedient people.'"

(Al-Ma'idah: 22-29).[1]

During the fourth century (BC) if you were to travel across the world, you would see people in small villages and towns living peacefully until the Greek armies of Alexander the Great, conquered, slaughtered and massacred innocent people. Ancient history of Philip II of Macedonia, followed by his son, Alexander the *So-Called Great* of Greece, led a series of army campaigns that killed and murdered people from the Adriatic Sea to the Indus River. Unfortunately, Alexander's polytheism military operations cease as a series of civil wars tore his empire apart after his short life and death in Babylon 323 BC but his paganism Hellenistic civilization continued.

The Roman Republic aggressively established its supremacy over the great powers such as Carthage, the Hellenistic kingdoms of Macedonia (Greeks), Syracuse (Italy) and the Seleucid Empire (Persia). From 247-183 BC, Hannibal Barca the great general and commander-in-chief of Carthage, Tunisia had no choice but to fight. During the second Punic war, Hannibal marched an army, which

---

[1] Quran: chapter 5

included war elephants, into Spain, over the Pyrenees and the Alps into Northern Italy. He won three major victories, however, while waiting for reinforcement, and occupying Italy for 15 years, a Roman general by the name of Scipio Africanus studied Hannibal's war tactics. Scipio planned a counter-invasion of North Africa and forced Hannibal to return to Carthage where he was decisively defeated in the Battle of Zama. Many African people do not know that Africa is named after this Italian man, Scipio Africanus.

The Greeks rose to power quickly and then dissolved quickly, but the next conqueror, the Romans, ruled for many years. The quest of the white Europeans to dominate, conquer, kill and destroy was insane. In Sub-Sahara Africa, one must ask, what were these ancient people doing? Because their history is oral, little is known about whether they successfully dominated and conquered each other. These people lived in small villages and tribes where they worshipped many deities and lived on the land as hunters and gatherers. Perhaps they were able to live in peace, devoid of aggression because of the climate. We can draw comparisons with the people of Sub-Saharan Africa to the Asian people who also lived without aggression, in harmony with their beliefs, philosophies and lifestyles. What is it about the white Europeans that makes them seek dominance and destruction? The Quran says God created man last; the animal kingdom, the plant kingdom and the world, in general, needed a head start before mankind came.

Behold, thy Lord said to the angels: "I will create

A vicegerent on earth." They said: "Wilt Thou place

Therein one who will make mischief therein and Shed blood? While we do celebrate Thy praises and Glorify Thy Holy (name)?" He said, "I know what you know not," 30 And He taught Adam the nature of things: then He placed them before the angels and said: tell Me the nature of these if ye are right." 31 [2](**Al -Baqarah***: 30-31)*

The angels serve as mankind's audience.   As witnesses to God's creation, they were vigilant to the actions and vice of man. Within the short amount of time that it took for God to create the animal and plant kingdoms, the angels grew bored. Immediately after God created Adam and Eve, they disobeyed God's orders. They fell from the heavens and earth caught them. They had children and one son, Cain who murdered his brother Abel out of jealousy. The angels love this action, it is the "mischief" that they asked God for. God created the devil and now the world has vices and sins like murder, anger, greed, sodomy, envy, pride, gluttony, slander, stealing, and more. These vices are present in all human beings and man must learn to control himself. It is not easy to practice self-control and the angels love to see mankind transgressing beyond bounds, hurting, killing and making

---

[2] Quran chapter 2

life difficult for each other. The angels are always in observance, laughing at the aggressive white people because they initiated the situation. Whites caused the mischief and continue to spill peoples' blood from ancient times to the present. The angels asked God to create something that would cause mischief and His answer to their prayers was the white man. And the Angels and the Jinn laugh at the white race because they know God will punish these creatures for their sinful actions in Hell!

Although the Western people are essential followers and believers of the aggressive Ibrahimic faiths, the Far East faiths of Hinduism and Buddhism are not known to be aggressive. Based on history, Hinduism is the oldest religion in the world, it is considered a polytheistic religion because it has over a hundred different gods and they also worship nature. The religion was founded in India and is strictly for Indians because they are the only people that can understand the language, practices (karma), philosophies, laws of daily morality and the dharma. If you visit India you will surely see big cows living in the street like civilians. Buddhism also started in the subcontinent of India around the 6th and 4th centuries BCE. Buddhism is mostly found in China and South East Asia. They follow the philosophy of Buddha, and it is taught that children should strive to be more successful than their parents. They are pure idol-worshipping people. Many Buddhist people put fruit in front of the big fat Buddha idol as though he will eat this fruit or will grant them success. These two faiths are more of a philosophy than a God faith-based religion. Another fact about Hinduism and Buddhism is that they are not aggressive religions like the Ibrahimic religions. Lastly, they did not spread to neighboring countries forcing the people to convert to their faith. Their history is not Hindus fighting Hindus or Buddhists fighting Buddhists, unlike the Jews, Christians and Muslims fighting within each other as well as each other and converting each other.

The pagan Roman Empire of ancient times, through conquest and assimilation, came to dominate southern Europe, Asia Minor, North Africa and parts of Eastern Europe by using their gods for help. These pagan people were able to lead successful war campaigns because they had a very organized autocratic government with senators for the legislature, good leadership and war generals. The Roman Empire first defeated the Greeks and the Gauls (France), then eventually they conquered northern Africa but Egypt proved to be difficult. Although Romans ruled, the Hellenistic cultures were the civilization of the ancient era from 323 BC to 30 BC (or arguably as late as 300 CE) left over from Alexander the Great triumphs. The Greek gods of Olympianism were worshiped, Egyptian gods were Isis and Serapis, and Syrian gods were Atargatis and Hadad, they helped people seek fulfillment in both life and the afterlife. In Egypt, the worship of rulers who were simply human beings factored into their practice of polytheism. Magic was practiced as well and people consulted oracles and used charms and figurines to determine misfortunes or to cast spells. The practice of astrology sought to determine a person's character and future in the movement of the sun, moons and stars.

Where are the divisions and sects in the pagan philosophies of the Hellenistic period? Did pagan sects fight each other and did one sect show superiority over the other? Well the one and only Ibrahim faith of this time, Judaism, had sects. The Pharisees (the oral law and Mosaic authority), the Sadducees (priestly privileges), the Essenes (who were pacifists or hate war and loved peace) and later the Zealots or military Jews were divided by their schools of thought. They had a Nation and lost it; the temple of Solomon was built then destroyed and rebuilt. During this time, Jews experienced slavery, anarchic and theocratic self-government, conquest, occupation, and exile. The Diasporas, have been in contact with and have been influenced by ancient Egyptian, Babylonian, Persian, and Hellenistic cultures. The Jewish people were ruled by Egyptian Ptolemaic and Hellenistic cultures that touched them; however, they could not mix with the infidels and would not convert them. Lastly, hostile neighbors were always on the verge of attacking them. This is the downfall of the Jewish people. They are told, "They are the chosen people" that the Ibrahim religion is only for them, and an individual has to be born a Jew. If you could see the good practicing Jews of the era and see the Hellenistic people, there is a great distinction that we see today.

Surely to win a war, it takes luck, weaponry, strategy, knowing one's enemy's strengths and weaknesses, smart tactical generals and ultimately help from God. The Jews needed lots of help they set themselves up to be hated and this is why their temple was destroyed. In history when it comes to religion there is no logic. The Jews put a Babylonian pagan king, Nebuchadnezzar II, in the Hebrew Bible. In 597 BC he invaded Judah, captured Jerusalem, destroyed Solomon's temple, deposed its King Jehoiakim and forced thousands of Jews into exile to Babylon (present-day Iraq). If Nebuchadnezzar II hated the Jews and their faith, why did he send them to his country (Iraq) to live? Next is Cyrus the Great, the Persian Zoroastrian ruler, he takes Babylon in 539 BC and allowed the Jewish elites to return to Jerusalem. They rebuilt their temple and were happy and at peace until Alexander the Great conquered them in 337 BC. Jews reluctantly accepted the Zoroastrian culture but they were forced to accept the polytheistic Greek culture or Hellenism. Ptolemaic, an Egyptian, one of Alexander the Great, generals ruled over Judea and the Temple. The empire of Egypt gave the Jews many civil liberties and they lived content under their rule. However, the Ptolemaic army was defeated in 198 BC at Panium by Antiochus III of the Seleucids. Antiochus wanted to Hellenize the Jews and make them worship the Greek gods and put them in the Temple. The Jews were forced to stop practicing many of their rituals; in turn, religious traditions were changed and they started making sacrifices to the Greeks gods. This was very offensive to the Ibrahim faith so the Jews revolted. They had no power, they fell susceptible to being conquered every 100 years and the conqueror's faith prevailed on the temple mount. It is not easy to practice your faith if you are ruled by another ethnicity that dislikes you and your beliefs. This is the situation with the first group of the Ibrahimic faith. The temple mount is seen as an icon in the ancient era and as well as today. The dominating faith is the faith you see on the mount. Jewish people understand the world and understand their faith, particularly the laws and the first commandment. They could not succumb to Hellenism, paganism or any polytheism. They had no choice but to fight and die for their beliefs. They battled the empire of Seleucid; God gave them this victory maybe because of their bravery, courage and faith, also the result of the war is the festival of Hanukkah. However, the unmerciful pagan Romans were next to conquer.

The Roman Republic and the Roman Empire were purely the most dominant white group of European people in the ancient era. 202 BC. Scipio Africanus defeated Hannibal and named Africa after himself. Rome annexed Spain, enslaved its own people of Apulia, and controlled Basilica Porcia and Aquileia Italy. The Gaul (France) was subjugated and Perseus was defeated (The Greeks) in the third Macedonian war. Also, when all of these countries revolted or rebelled against being enslaved and or subordinated, the Roman military returned and massacred/slaughtered them. The Lusitania rebelled (Portugal) and the Celts of Spain destroyed Corinth a city in Greece and destroyed Carthage in 146 BC (Tunisia) crucified 4,500 slaves in the first Servile wars, Spartacus revolted in the third servile war. Crassus, a Roman general and politician suppressed Spartacus's gladiators' revolt and 6,000 slaves were crucified on the Via Appea in 71 BC. Marius defeated Jugurtha, King of Numida and the Berbers of North Africa (Algeria). Next in line is the tyrant, Julius Caesar. He fought the German tribes, crushed the revolt in Gaul, and invaded Britain. Germany was his next stop, followed by Egypt where he also seduced Queen Cleopatra (ethnically a Macedonian). What is it that the Romans promoted? Did they spread Hellenism to this western area of the world? Did they want money or gold? Are they so successful because they have excellent military power, weaponry, ruthless senators, and unmerciful generals and tyrant politicians? Surely these are all white dominating people.

Are God's angels happy, are their eyes seeing, getting enough action? Professional soldiers killing innocent people, corrupt politicians, perverted sex, and all the vices are in action, all the sins were being practiced, and the devil's plan is in full force. There was only one group on the face of the earth that worshipped God properly and their faith was weak and constantly challenged. Before being defeated and killed by the Parthian Empire (Persians), at the battle of Carrhae (Syria), Roman general, Crassus stopped at Jerusalem and desecrated the temple. A chapter in the Quran entitled, "The Romans" states, "The Romans were defeated but soon they should have victory." Cyrus the great, a fire worshiping Zoroastrian from Persia, helped the Israelites return to Jerusalem and rebuild their temple. However, Roman generals were responsible for destroying the temple multiple times. Pagans, the Romans demonstrated no respect for the monotheistic religion of Judaism, so they tried their best to depopulate and disgrace them. For some reason, the Arab people and God favor the pagan Roman Empire over fire worshiping Zoroastrian Persians. The Romans never attempted to conquer Arabia because of the terrain and climate.

Finally, we have arrived at the end of the 1st millennium BC era where the civil war took place in the republic, Julius Caesar was assassinated by Marcus Brutus (a politician of the late Roman Republic in 42BC) and the senators participated in perverted sex orgies. Marcus Antonius divorced his wife, Octavian and married Cleopatra. Together, Marcus and Cleopatra fought the Roman Empire in the battle of Actium where they faced defeat. At the end of the civil wars, Marcus and Cleopatra committed suicide and Egypt became annexed to the Roman Empire. Herod the *so-called* Great, became the client King of Judea and gave birth to Herod Antipas the Tetrarch ("ruler of a quarter"), who is best known for the beheading of "John the Baptist" and the alleged execution of Jesus Christ.

Chapter II

Christ, Jesus "the Son of Mariam"

Jesus was the word of God
The disciples were true believers of Jesus
Paul was the devil's advocate
Roman Emperors murdered Judeo-Christians
Constantine created the Christianity
The concept of the Holy trinity
which became another form of polytheism

Jesus Christ was born just like every human being. A born prophet, he was the son of Mariam and a true believer in the God of Ibrahim from the genealogy of Jacob, Isaac and Ibrahim, based on the Quran and the Bible. Zachariah, a priest, a believer, a Prophet, the father of John the Baptist and the husband of Elisabeth, who is the cousin of Mary whom he took care of. Zachariah prayed to God to have a child that would not be tempted by the devil. Elisabeth became pregnant with John through natural conception. Mary, on the other hand, was impregnated with Jesus by the "Holy Spirit" after she received a visit from the archangel', "Gabriel." He not only told Mary that she would have a son, but he revealed to her the name that her son would carry. It is this "Holy Spirit" that strengthens Jesus' soul, fortifying him against temptation, most importantly making Him the spoken word of God and also the answer to Zachariah's prayer.

Based on Jesus' genealogy, he was qualified to preach in the temple of Solomon and to give new covenants. God gave His prophet the extraordinary task of being the Messiah. Jesus' first mission was to make the Israelites practice the Mosaic Law, forming them into one believing group. The Jews remained the only people in the world that worshipped God the right way but they were surrounded by the influence of pagan people. They have been ruled and persecuted by the Hellenistic rulers of the Roman Empire and Greeks. Jesus was sent to the Jewish people to put them back on the straight path to God so that they could receive His Mercy. In doing so, Jesus ran into many obstacles: Herod the Great and his son, rulers of Judea and Jerusalem, the pagan Roman Empire and lastly, his own feeble-minded Jewish brethren.

Based on who reads the Bible and interprets it you can see that Jesus came to and preached to Jewish people only.

> *(1): "And when he had called unto him his twelve disciples, he gave them power against unclean spirits, to cast them out, and to heal all manner of sickness and all manner of disease. (2): Now the names of the twelve apostles are these:...(5)These twelve Jesus sent forth and commanded them, saying, Go not into the way of the Gentiles and into any city of the Samaritans enter ye not (6): but go rather to the lost sheep of the house of Israel (7)And as ye go preach saying 'The kingdom of heaven is at hand'" (Matthews 10)* [3]

---

[3] Bible: Matthews

Know that Jesus is referred to as the prophet of Nazareth in the books of Matthew, Mark, John, and Luke. Jesus was a Prophet whose message spoke negatively of the Gentile peoples. Jesus viewed Gentiles as being unclean because they did not practice the Jewish custom of circumcision. However, if a Gentile wanted to convert and accept Judaism's customs, covenants and laws, they were welcome. Jesus did not preach in a church, nor did he have churches established in his time. All of his disciples were Jewish men. As the Messiah, he was intended to be the ruler or king of his people. This did not bode well with King Herod the Great and his son Antipus. Herod wanted to end Jesus' life at birth out of fear that the Roman Empire's rule was challenged. Jesus, Mary and his stepfather Joseph moved to Egypt to live then up North to Nazareth, Palestine where he spoke Aramaic.

Jesus had a large following. The early followers did not worship Jesus, nor did Jesus tell them he was the son of God or God. It would have been considered blasphemous if Jesus told the people that he was God. If Jesus allowed his followers to worship him, they would all be in a state of sin. Jesus practiced and believed in the Mosaic laws and his teachings focused particularly on the first one, "Thou shalt have no God but Thee." One must be very careful when reading material about Jesus written by Christians. Christians' opinion began in 325 AD Roman Catholicism, established by the Nicaea council and the white dominating rulers of that time. With the insanity of the Christian writers and their ignorance in understanding

God's scriptures, the population at the end of Jesus' mission were two the minority of weak Israelites that Jesus came to and the majority Hellenistic the many gods worshiping pagan people. There is no scripture in the New Testament that confirms that Jesus Christ came to the Jews and gentiles to save them from their sins.

Because Jesus did not complete his mission, he will return. Believe it or not, the God of Ibrahim is in control, and He knows what He is doing. Jesus was created in a special way because God wanted to show him the earth only to test the people and then take him from the earth and bring him back at the end of time. These are pure faith-based statements believe it or not the word, the Book. Should the people believe in white legislators, and emotional clergy men and go to hell? When Jesus returns, his greatest obstacle will be the Christian people who believe in the trinity and have their many churches, denominations, sects, their worldly dominates, white persuasion, the violent nature of white people, the arrogant person who lives at 1600 Pennsylvania and worse they worship him breaking the first commandment. It may be very difficult for white Christians to cleanse their blasphemous souls. However, the prophet Muhammad said that many Christians will convert to Islam during the second coming of Jesus Christ as the people did when Islam was first introduced.

Christians can criticize Hindus for their belief in reincarnation that suggesting that a human can return to another life as an animal. Hindus have the right to challenge the Christian idea of worshipping a white man they call Jesus in the idolatrous form of pictures and sculptures. Hindus think the Islamic faith is ridiculous because Muslims worship a God that they have never seen.

The Catholic Church claims that it was founded circa 30 AD. Fact one, there were no Catholic Churches in 30 AD. Fact two, Jesus Christ absolutely did not preach in a church. Jesus was not ready for the complicity of that era and society. Jesus' mission was not to wage war, he preached against hatred and violence, not like the Christians of today. Historically, Jewish people have been resistant to change. The Jewish ruler Herod, also a practicing Jew, falsely accused Jesus of the crime of being the Messiah. Notwithstanding the lack of knowledge of King Herod, Jesus is the one who will return or "the Messiah." Pilate, the Roman governor of Israel was responsible for making the determination whether Jesus was innocent or guilty. Pilate, Herod, Judas, Annas, Caiaphas and the entire Sanhedrin, the Supreme Court of Israel were all detrimental figures in Jesus' tragic life on earth. All of these men thought that they had the power or the influence to determine the destiny of Jesus by rendering judgment. In reality, the destiny of Jesus had long been determined by God. Jesus was not the victim of a corrupt disciple that betrayed him. He was not the victim of a couple of corrupt High Priests who arraigned him. He was not the victim of the Jewish Supreme Court who condemned him. Nor was he the victim of Pilate and

Herod who ultimately executed him. He was God's chosen Lamb, and God predetermined that He would leave the earth, however, will return in the near future.

The pagan Roman Empire still rules the world. Jesus' followers and disciples did not provide Jesus with moral support as witnesses or friends during his persecution. At this time in Jesus' life, Paul was in another city working for the Roman Empire, plotting the persecution of Jesus Christ's followers.

Does the introduction of a new Prophet signify the need for a new religion? Jesus came to preach the laws to Jews who refused to comply, but in return reached a mass of people who actually believed in his teachings. Many Jews continued to practice the same Judaism as though Jesus never came. The Judeo-Christian period that took place after Jesus' left the earth, is when some followers accepted him as a Prophet, thus deeming them Judeo-Christian. However, Paul preached that Jesus was God and the son of God. Paul stated that he received a revelation from Jesus in the form of a very bright light that blinded him. Paul depicted this story in the New Testament, in the book of Acts and in other books. The other disciples challenged Paul very little. James, "the just," disagreed with Paul about the gentiles practicing the law. Paul was considered to be a zealot Jew or a militant. He was clever, aggressive and determined to indoctrinate many people with the new faith that he created. Hellenistic pagan people had been practicing Greco-Roman polytheism for over 300 years and they were ignorant of the Jewish laws and practices. This made it easy for Paul to tell them that Jesus was a god. Egyptian Pharaohs and some Roman Caesars considered themselves gods and the people revered these leaders as such. Through Paul, Jesus became an idol. Why did the 12 Jewish disciples allow one man to destroy Jesus' mission and message? The first commandment was negated by Paul.

Ibrahim fulfilled all the commandments and trials which God tried him over his lifetime. Ibrahim was a prophet and apostle of God and patriarch of many people. God promised Ibrahim, that he would be a leader to all the nations of the world and his sons would have nations. Before Ibrahim's death, he instilled in his sons to solely worship God as One. The believers only had to worship God in theory. Moses was different from his Israelites because now the believers had the written law, some rituals and prayer. The same with David and Solomon more written stories, practices, the Psalms and now they had a temple as a significant place to worship. Most important the Isaac side of the Ibrahim family received many Prophets to give guides to the believers and taught them how to worship and practice the faith correctly even though sects and separation came.

> *And who turns away from the religion*
> *of Abraham*
> *But such as debase their souls with*
> *folly? Him We chose*
> *And rendered pure in this world: and*
> *he will be in the hereafter in the ranks*
> *of the righteous. 131. Behold! His lord*

*said to him: "Bow (thy will to me):" He
said: "I bow (my will) to the lord and
cherisher Of the Universe." 132. And
this was the legacy that Abraham left to
his son
And so did Jacob; "Oh my son! God
hath chosen the Faith for you; Then die
not except in the faith of Islam." 133.
Were ye witness when death appeared
before Jacob? Behold, he said to his
sons: "What will ye worship after me?"
They said: "We shall worship Thy God
and the God of thy Fathers, Of
Abraham, Ismail, and Isaac, the One
(True) God:
To Him we bow (in Islam)." 135. They
say: "Become Jews or Christians if ye
would be guided (to salvation)." Say
thou "Nay! (I would rather) the
Religion of Abraham the True, And he
joined not gods with God." 136.
Say ye: "We believe in God, and the
revelation Given to us, and to Abraham,
Ismail, Isaac, Jacob, And the Tribes,
and given to Moses and Jesus, And that
given to (all) Prophets from their Lord:
We make no difference between one and
another Of them: and we bow to God
(in Islam) 137. So if they believe as ye
believe, they are indeed on the right
path; but if they turn back, it is they
who are in schism; but God will suffice
thee as against them, And He is the All-
Hearing, the All-Knowing. (**Al-
Baqarah 130-137**)*[4]

It is apparent that Christianity and Judaism do not have the same beginnings. Although Jesus was born a Jewish man, from a Jewish mother the Christian people worshipped him. Jesus is not the founder of Christianity. If he was the founder, believers would have a complete understanding of how to practice the faith. The Council of Nicaea in 325 AD would not be necessary to attain consensus, create a trinity and establish an Easter holiday. Hundreds of Christians would not have different beliefs and there would have been no need for Roman Catholic heresy. Christianity was a formless faith that could not lay claim to a church, its own religious text, no prophet, and no prayer. There was no correct understanding of belief; practices, rituals, and covenants were established by one man, Paul.

Saul of Tarsus was Paul's Jewish name. Saul was a zealot Jew employed by the Roman Empire to persecute the followers of Jesus Christ. In the time of Jesus, there was no Christianity. Jesus did not call his followers Christians. A very important fact is that Paul never met Jesus, and he never saw Jesus either. Paul was not a disciple of Jesus and certainly not a servant of God. Paul asserted himself as the apostle to the gentile people. Having a strong personality, he was educated, clever and very aggressive. He places himself in the company of the disciples like Simon, Peter, James the Just and Barnabas. Paul was not qualified to write the New Testament. It is

---

[4] Quran: Al Baqarah

said that Paul was struck blind by the resurrected Jesus who was illuminated by a great light. On the day that Jesus was nailed on the cross, no one witnessed a great light beaming from the earth to the sky; God raised Jesus' soul into the heavens before Jesus ever made it to the cross. If Paul was alive he would have written many successful movie scripts and books because Paul managed to produce fourteen epistles in the New Testament. Modern scholars question Paul's contradicting stories because there is no consistency and authenticity.

Paul created and founded Christianity for the Gentiles of the Hellenist world and the Roman Empire. He preached that Jesus is the son of God and he died for everyone's sins. He actually changed and countered everything that Jesus stood for. In Paul's Christianity, there is no more Mosaic law, no more rituals, no more dietary teaching and no more work (prayer, fasting, sacrifice and pilgrimage). Salvation is achieved by simply believing that Jesus died for the sins of man on the cross and was resurrected. This is a very false and dangerous covenant. The Gentile people were destined to go to hell based on their pagan beliefs, and their rejection of the Ibrahimic faith. Thanks to Paul, they continued on their route to hell because they continued to break the first commandment of the Mosaic Laws.

With one more visit to Jerusalem in 70 AD, Paul's Gentile religion grew although the Roman Empire began to persecute the people of this new faith. One must admire the guts and determination of the Jews to be independent of Hellenism and Roman pagan dominance. The Great Revolt or the first Jewish war (66-73 CE) again the Roman Empire from the eyes of a Roman officer fighting a war again religious people that you dislike was far more different from the fight the nation of the Persians that they also dislike. After the defeat, the Romans forced the Jews to leave Jerusalem. Many fled to Egypt, Iraq, Iran, and Arabia while the Temple was destroyed again. Titus, a Roman Emperor distinguished himself as a skilled general after he successfully invaded and destroyed the city and Temple of Jerusalem. Josephus, a Jewish writer and betrayer survived a group suicide of 960 Jewish rebels and their families (the siege of Masada by the troops of the Roman Empire). He was able to write about the Masada and while imprisoned, he wrote that he provided the Romans with intelligence on the ongoing revolt. It may be better to let your enemy murder, kill, slaughter, massacre the people and die a martyr than to commit suicide.

A new prophet ushered in a new religion. The Jews and the Judeo-Christians were not shining and neither was Judaism or Christianity. Maybe in the eyes of God, these persecuted believers are shining. The Hellenist pagan people did not want to convert to Judaism. Perhaps Paul understood their reluctance. Paul was not a faithful Jew and he did not see it necessary to properly practice all Jewish laws and rituals. Was it God's intention to wean the Hellenistic pagans from their practice of idolatry and make them dependent on a false version of Ibrahimic faith

(Paul's Christian) until the ultimate truth comes with the next Prophet?

The disciples of Jesus (Peter, Andrew, James, John, Philip, Bartholomew, Thomas, Matthew, James, Jude, Simon, and Matthias replaced Judas) were men of God and believers in the God of Ibrahim and Jesus as the Prophet says, "the Quran." They were all persecuted and died as martyrs; they all went to different foreign countries to preach the gospel. Reading about the apostles from their perspective is very vague. To say they all preached the gospel is vague. It is certain that Peter, Paul and Barnabas were not in agreement on what to preach and who to preach to. In the first hundred years of Christianity, there is no New Testament, no doctrine and most importantly, no orthodox. The end result is that Christianity was not a uniform religion. Egypt believed different from the people in Jerusalem, people in Jerusalem believed different from people in Syria, people in Syria believed different from people in Rome, Greece and on and on. Within the Roman Empire, all of the churches preached a different doctrine and delivered different messages which confused the ignorant Gentile people. History does not say that any apostle started any of the following churches: the Roman Catholic Church, Greek Orthodox Church, the Eastern Church or Anglican Church. The word veneration is very weak, they say it from their mouth but show no proof or fact. The fact is that all of the apostles were Judeo-Christian people who practiced the laws and did not believe in any trinity and or break the first three commandments.

A little story from the Hadith, after the death of Muhammad, a Sahaba in the company of another Sahaba's (a person that knew the prophet, learn from him, believed in the message and put it into practice) this man said, "let worship Muhammad like the Christians worship there Prophet," Abu Badr, the sitting Caliph said, "the Quran states that Muhammad is an Abdullah (servant of God) therefore if anybody worship's Muhammad, I'm going to take his head off grabbing his sword." And that was the end of that. Maybe if Jesus' disciples, because they were true believers after hearing that Paul was changing the word, the creed and practice of Jesus; the disciples should have taken stronger actions against Paul to stop the Blasphemy by taking his head off. (**Hadith**)[5]

On the streets of the new millennium (the first three hundred years of this new faith), the people knew that Jesus was a human being, that he was not God. Christianity spread by word of mouth, a demonstration of a lack of knowledge and ignorance. Many learned men devised many ways and scenarios of how to believe and worship the two and three god conception. Notwithstanding there was never one Christianity in the whole history of this faith. Why? Because Jesus is not the founder of the faith and is not the Prophet of the faith and the people who followed Paul were led astray. After Paul, many sects of Christianity were created. The believers

---

[5] Hadith

were oppressed and persecuted by the Roman Emperors, 10 of the 12 disciples were crucified, and no realistic apostolic succession ever occurred. The Bible was not published as a book until 500 years after Jesus. The people who called themselves Christians had no source of reference and many were illiterate. Finally, the white people of the Pagan Roman Empire continued to seek dominance and managed to conquer countries around the Mediterranean Sea. There are three religious groups: the people who follow the God of Ibrahim (Monotheists), the people who follow Paul (Christians) and the pagans.

And in the 4th century when the Roman Empire accepts Pauline's Christianity or the Trinity this will end the era of Jewish Christianity and started the era of white Christian domination.

A list of some of the early sects and what their theory and beliefs were:

Sabellianism founded Sabellius in the 2nd century as a presbyter in Rome. It is sometimes referred to as modalistic Monarchianism. Sabellius states that the father, son, and Holy Ghost are three modes, roles, or faces of a single person, God. This, of course, implies that Jesus Christ was purely divine, without humanness, and therefore could not truly have suffered or died.

Docetism or the Gnostic, the meaning "to seem," he says that Christ was not a real human being did not have a real human body and did he suffer. He only seemed to be human to us.

Monophysitism means "one body," They say that Jesus Christ (two separate natures human and divine) joined in one body. Monophysitism is very much alive practiced by Coptics in present-day Egyptian, Syria and Middle Eastern sects of Christianity.

Adoptionism says that Jesus was a human being born of Joseph and Mary. Another theory Jesus was "adopted" by God at his conception, and after being baptized by John the Baptist who developed a divine nature.

Nestorianism the founder Nestorius, Patriarch of Antioch (fl. 410), believed that Jesus Christ had two natures -- man and God – or the man Jesus and the divine Son of God.

Apollinarianism the founder Apollinaris of Laodicea (fl. 350), says that Jesus Christ was not a real man, but not totally divine either. Apollinarians suggested that he had a human body and a human soul, but his mind was taken over by the eternal Logos.

Arianism the founder Arius (c. 250 - c. 336), a priest in Alexandria states that Jesus Christ was thought of as a special creation by God for man's salvation. Arianism was the form of Christianity that the Goths adhered to, and it was popular in all the areas they conquered, including Italy, Spain, and Africa.

Socianism founder Faustus Socinus simply says that Jesus was an extraordinary man. Also an offshoot of Arianism, today they are two very different forms, the Unitarians and the Jehovah's Witnesses.

Not all heresies focused on the issues of the trinity and Christ's nature. Here are the leading examples.

Donatism: Named for its leader, the theologian Donatus the Great (d. 355), Donatism included a group of extremist sects, mostly in North Africa, that emphasized asceticism. They valued martyrdom, found lapses of faith (even under torture or threat of death) inexcusable, and believed that the sacraments required a pure priest to be effective.

Pelagianism: Another group of sects, centered in Gaul, Britain, and Ireland, are associated with the Irish monk Pelagius (fl. 410). He believed that original sin was not transmitted from Adam and Eve to their children (and thereby to us). Baptism was not considered necessary, and people could be "saved" by their own efforts, that is, they did not necessarily require the grace of God. Many modern liberal Christians agree with Pelagius.

Gnosticism: the Roman philosophy and their religion mixed with Christian versions were, obviously, considered serious heresies. Gnosticism has never entirely disappeared, and can be seen in the traditions of Alchemy and Astrology, and even in modern times in the works of Carljung.

Manicheanism: Manicheanism is actually a separate religion that blends Christianity with Gnosticism, Mithraism, neo-Platonism, and even Buddhism. Again, it was considered a very serious heresy. It survived well into the middle Ages, where it strongly influenced the Bogomils in the Balkans and the Cathars in southern France.

The Bulgarian Heresy:

The Bogomils and the Cathars were harshly persecuted by the Orthodox Church in the east and the Catholic Church in the west. By the 14th century, the Bulgarians were absorbed by the Islamic Ottoman Empire, and the Cathars were virtually eliminated by the Crusades and the Inquisition. They had laid the foundations, however, for the Reformation.[6]

This writer defines heresy as a belief that deviates from the standard, official belief but there is no standard official belief in Christianity because of the three or two gods conception and the nature of Jesus. The foundation of Christianity was never manifested in the land because of all the deaths of the 12 disciples. The end results were ignorant men to follow. Know that all of the Heresies are named after the man that started that type of church and heresy. Again, the biggest problem with Christianity is hear-say. Too many writers and the entire so-called scroll offered no help to the Bishops' understanding of Christianity. The Bible is written by many different men and many gospels convey different stories. Which one is telling the truth, which one is inspired by God? Finally, the Bible leaves people in doubt, no certainty there is

---

[6] Internet: webspace.ship.edu

absolutely any verse in the Bible to back up the trinity and of Jesus being the son of god.

When the Pagan Roman Empire grew exhausted from persecuting the Christians, the emperor Constantine became the first Roman Emperor to convert to Christianity circa 320 AD. Constantine gave the people a sense of religious tolerance. Constantine acknowledged that members of the Christian sects were large in number so he formed the first Council of Nicaea (in Turkey) in an effort to attain consensus in the church through an assembly representative of all Christendom.

Really! The end result of Jesus coming and going is the belief in the trinity, the implementation of the Easter holiday, the formation of Roman Catholicism, and the start of this book, "White Christian Domination: When Will it End"?

Chapter III

The Start of White Christian domination

The Prophet Jesus preached no hatred, no violence,
He never forced a gentile to convert or
accused his believers of heresy
White Christianity distributed evil around the world
Under the guise of a man-made dogma

Did the Roman Empire accept Christianity or did they create their own version of Christianity with Catholicism? Catholicism was created in 325 AD by Constantine I and the Council of Nicaea. There is a significant lapse in time between the 12 disciples and the start of Catholicism. None of the 12 disciples were Catholics, none of them believed in the trinity and not one of these men ever visited or preached in a church. When Roman Catholicism became the official religion of the Roman Empire, the issue and practice of heresy were rampant. Under the control of the Roman Empire, Christian people had to consider themselves Catholic if they wished to avoid punishment for heresy. Everyone was forced to believe in the Roman Catholic Church and its dogma. Consequently, from the fourth century on, not only did emperors organize councils to address heresy, but they also established a wide range of civil penalties. These penalties consisted of fines, imprisonment and capital punishment.

With the initiation of Roman Catholicism, this religion became the orthodox practice of Christianity. It needs to be understood that the pagan Roman Empire created Roman Catholicism. This religion was purely man-made! Once this is comprehended, one can see how people have been controlled by this religion. We can look to the Catholic Bible as an example to see how the Roman Empire determined which gospels to use and destroy in order to create dogma.

Let's venture back to the BC period and calculate the human lives that were lost because of conquests made by Alexander the Great, the Persian Empire and the Roman Empire. Approximately 10 million people died during these horrific times of white dominance and the number continues to grow because man does not understand the meaning of peace.

When the early Christians built their church, they did not see the significance of building the church on the temple mount. However, they did erect the Sepulchre Church where it is believed that Jesus was resurrected. The church is presently shared by the Greek Orthodox, Eastern Orthodox, Oriental Orthodox, the Roman Catholic Church, Anglicans, and Non-Trinitarians; thus leaving the Protestant Christians without a presence in the church.

During this period in history, the Eastern and Roman Catholic Churches both claim to be the orthodox faith, laying claim to being the one holy, Catholic and Apostolic Church. The Assyrian church also claims to be the original orthodox faith, claiming that they were founded by the apostle, Peter. Before the first Council of Nicaea, these three orthodox churches had three different theologies and practices. Is Peter responsible for disseminating three different beliefs, doctrines and dogmas?

Why does the Christian faith need a governing body like the Council of Nicaea to determine systematic belief? The reason behind this is that the Bible is not the word of Jesus or God, but the words of many different men. In addition, the concept of the trinity will always be difficult for men to agree on a universal interpretation. The birth of Jesus and the way he left the earth are all miraculous events and these ignorant men should have left it at that.

The Roman Catholic Church attempted to erase all of the heresy that took place under the Council of Nicaea in 325 AD. The first council that was formed is the blame for the confusion revolving around Christianity. Although the concept of the trinity is not supported by the Bible all of the orthodox churches (Eastern Orthodox, Oriental Orthodox, Assyrian, Anglicans, Roman Catholics as well as the Protestants) accepted the doctrine. The erroneous foundation of Christianity was promoted by the Council of Nicaea and people followed the dogma that the council created. The followers should have asserted themselves and said, "I accept, believe and practice only the teachings of Jesus." But without legitimate documents and gospels to establish their own dogma, they could rely on nothing but their experience and false leaders like Paul. This is a clear picture of the state of the church in the 4th century, easily persuaded and vulnerable to the ulterior motives of

Constantine and the Roman Empire. Discussion and debates took place concerning the trinity. Athanasius, a bishop and theologian of Alexandria, Egypt and Arius, a theologian and ascetic Christian presbyter also of Alexandria, Egypt are popular proponents of support and opposition. Athanasius believed that the three godheads in the trinity were all equal in power and significance. However, Arius opposed the trinity. His arguments place emphasis on God's divinity as the Father. As the creator of all, God created the Son of God as a distinct individual we know as Jesus. He supported his creed with scripture from John 14:28. As a consequence of Arius' assertions, Emperor Constantine denounced Arius as a heretic, burnt his books and excommunicated him from the Roman Catholic Church. The foundation of Christianity depended on two men, Athanasius and Arius, not the teachings of Jesus Christ or even his disciples.

During the second Council of Constantinople (381 AD), the controversial Arian concept was still in the minds of the masses. Arius' debate about the definition of the trinity continued. Simultaneously, all four orthodox churches within the Roman Empire continued to preach different messages. Constantine soon began to regret the decision he made with the first Nicene Council. He granted amnesty to the Arian leaders and exiled Athanasius because of Eusebius of Nicomedia. Eusebius, the bishop that baptized Constantine, influenced the imperial family and favored Arius' theory over Athanasius'. Constantine was not the best judge for the fate of his people for he to accept the Arian creed at Baptism then change to the Athanasian Creed at the first council of Nicaea, and then change back to Arian theory. He was surely a baffled confused man.

Insanity never dissolves in this man-made religion, new individuals continued to promote new theories and doctrines. The teaching of Nestorius through Nestorianism emphasized the disunity between Christ's human and divine natures. So in 431 AD, the Council of Ephesus was created. Before the council condemned him as a heretic, a new god was created, Mary.

In 451 AD, the Council of Chalcedon debated the definition of Jesus Christ as God and as a man. The question was does Jesus have two natures? Churches were divided into many different premises revolving around Jesus' divinity, singularity, and how he was conceived. Like the Arian creed, this council concluded that Jesus Christ was human and divine in nature.

To end this chapter, the great Constantine I created the Roman Catholic Church and the trinity doctrine. He was the first to lead white Christians as a dominating force. When men sit down and talk and talk but show no new reference but their dominating forceful egotistical thoughts then the end result was war. In the 11th century after the Great Schism under Pope Leo IX, the unholy Holy Roman Empire (the Roman Catholic Church) used the merciless Crusaders to attack the Eastern Greek church in Turkey slaughtering thousands of Christian (also known as the Latin massacre of over 60,000 Eastern Orthodox

Christians were put to death by the sword). The Church was divided due to differences in doctrine, theology, linguistics, politics and geographical boundaries. The fundamental breach was never resolved with each side accusing the other of having fallen into heresy and of having initiated the division. And the madness continues the Catholic Church considers the Protestant denominations to be all heretical and the Eastern Orthodox Church considers both the Roman Catholic Church and the Protestant denominations to be heretical.

In the 13ᵗʰ century, dissenting opinions on how to distinguish heretics from the devout presented considerable difficulties. But, according to popular legend, the problem was solved by Arnaud, the papal legate. Arnaud instructed the crusaders with the following command, "Kill everyone! God will recognize His own!" Although the crusaders did their best to follow these instructions and exterminate the Albigenses (people of south France), this sort of wholesale butchery was impractical.

Saint Dominic, the founder of the Dominican order and the leader of "The Inquisition" led a group of decentralized institutions under the direction of the Roman Catholic Church to destroy all heresy. These ruthless people were convinced that they were fighting with the power of darkness for the prisoner's soul. A victim who died unrepentantly was a victory for the devil. One of the most terrible of men in the Inquisition was Conrad of Marburg, Germany. He created a reign of terror unrivaled by any tyrant until the advent of Hitler. Conrad forced confession, and torture and burned people at the stake. Under torture, entire families confessed and while under the threat of additional tortures, they implicated others. The accused were instantly arrested and tortured until they named others and soon half the population of Germany was under accusation. Many innocent Catholics were martyrs, choosing to be burned at the stake rather than confess to vicious crimes.

One event that cannot be ignored on the pages of Christian medieval history is the plague of witchcraft that terrorized Europe for centuries. In 1488 Pope Innocent VIII issued an infamous bill against witchcraft, ordering the Inquisition to stamp it out at all costs. He appointed James Sprenger, a German priest, as inquisitor-general. Sprenger accepted the post eagerly and considered virtually all mental abnormalities as being the work of the devil or of his agents, the witches. In Sprenger's famous book, *Malleus Malficarum,* he labeled people who suffer from compulsion neurosis, psychosis, and schizophrenia as witches. He described how the witches heard voices, had visions and how some were actually cured by torture. According to Sprenger, people with hysterical anesthesia and pathological mutism could be cured by "shock treatment". *Malleus Malficarum* was used for centuries after his death as the definitive text on witchcraft, providing a guide on how to secure confessions. This book is probably responsible for the death of more human beings than any other book in history. In W. F. Poole's book, *Salem Witchcraft,* he depicted how several thousand people were executed by Christian rulers for this "crime" during the 16th-18th centuries.

Surely while reading this chapter, the reader may think the subject matter is about criminals. Can we estimate the number of people that lose their lives from the barbaric actions of the Roman Catholic Church, their Popes, and kings? Next, the coming of the merciless Crusaders and their aggressive attack on the Muslim world, then the attack on the Eastern Orthodox Church in Turkey and Greece, the heresy throughout the Roman Empire and the European world will continue. Then came the inquisition; good estimation of over 20 million people between 100AD to 1500AD lost their lives. And surely the first Roman Catholic and or forced Christianize Massacre by the German Charlemagne in 782ad of over 4500 Saxons, Germanic paganism must be written. Is the Roman Catholic Church a place of faith or is it an organization of gangsters, who forces their dogma on the people of the world? There was absolutely no freedom of religion under the Roman Catholic Church in the Roman Empire and furthermore, there was never the word forgives in these people's hearts. The Jewish people through the Christian domain were in bondage and could not live under Christian leadership. Finally, if the Christian people were following the Prophet Jesus' personality, his character and his ethics and not worshiping him; perhaps they too would be non-violent, devoid of hatred, and have some mercy and sympathy for others. Unfortunately, this is not the case. White Christian domination was born and bred by Kings who used soldiers to distribute evil around the world, all the while thanking God for the conquests.

Chapter IV

The Burst of the truth

Do the people want the truth and follow
an illiterate Arab Prophet? Or do the
people want to follow White dominations
white legislations and
white educated clergymen

Roman worldwide rule continued through 600 AD. At war with the Persians, the believing people were oppressed by Roman Catholicism. There were still heresies in the empire, the Jews had no temple or nation, and Israel is still called Palestine. The Arab people in Arabia were never conquered by the Roman Empire, the Assyrians, the Babylonians, the Greeks and the Persian Empire. The Arabs mostly kept to themselves in the Arabian Peninsula where desert life was harsh, with frequently fought among themselves. It was the Islamic faith that gave the Arabs a sense of pride, bravery and determination to conquer and rule the world for a short period of time. The Arabian Muslims conquered the Romans in Palestine and the Persian Empire simultaneously. They dramatically changed the state, government, and education. Jews, Christians, Pagans and Zoroastrians were coerced to convert to Islam. Within 50 years, the Roman Empire's land mass in the Middle East and North Africa was Islamic. The people who understood the scripture in the Roman Empire were aware that another Prophet would be sent. Many Jews and

Christians accepted the Islamic faith's authenticity and provisions for life. Islam rapidly changed the culture, lifestyle, and outlook on the lives that the faith touched. People were able to revive peace and happiness without the aggression from the old ancient fronts (Romans, Persians, Syrians, Greeks, and Egyptians). Islam is very simple: belief in the One God, Muhammad the last Prophet, pray, fast, be charitable and make the pilgrimage to Mecca. Within the Masjid is where worship and Islamic education took place, devoid of paganism and idolatry, purifying people's minds and souls.

Muhammad is the descendant of Ishmael by way of Ibrahim. An Old Testament story depicts Ibrahim taking Hagar and their son Ishmael to Arabia. In Arabia, they built a house that became the "Kaaba" or the house of God. However, in the Old Testament Arabia, Mecca and Medina were all called by different names. Based on the scriptures, the Jews knew that the next prophet would come from Arabia. However, they did not know that he would be an Arabic descendant of Ishmael, not an Israelite descendant of Jacob and Isaac. Muhammad was of the Hashemite family and from the Quraish tribe which ruled and controlled the pagan people of Mecca. Muhammad entered Mt. Hira to be by himself far away from the unbelieving and wicked people. According to Islamic beliefs the archangel Gabriel first appeared to Muhammad in 610 AD in the form of a man. He embraced Muhammad saying, "Read, read." To which Muhammad replied, "I don't know how to read."

> Read [O Muhammad!] in the name of your Lord and Cherisher, who created. Created man out of a (mere) clot Of congealed blood. Read, and your Lord is the Most Bountiful, He who (taught the use of) the pen, taught man that which he knew not. (**Iqraa 96, 1-5**)[7]

Muhammad left the Mountain sweating bullets. His wife Khadijah greeted him upon his return and he told her about his experience. She sought the Christian priest for guidance and Muhammad recounted his experience with the angel, Gabriel. The priest said, "You must be the chosen one, the Prophet that would come after Jesus, the prophet for mankind." He asked Muhammad to tell him more and asked for further instruction. Muhammad did not know at the time. One of the significant attributes of the Islamic faith is that Muhammad, an illiterate Prophet, only took orders and revelations from the archangel Gabriel for the first 15 years of his prophethood. He did not elaborate or express his opinion on the many issues and questions that were coming from the hostile Arab people. The archangel Gabriel is the Holy Ghost in the bible; however, the term Holy Ghost is a false label by the unknowledgeable and ignorant authors of the bible. We are human beings with names and Gabriel is an 'Angel' and his name happens to be Gabriel. Calling Gabriel a Holy Ghost is an insult to this entity. The word Ghost means evil spirit. Holy is a positive adjective that modifies a negative

---

[7] Quran: chapter 96

word which demonstrates how white Christians use language to misinterpret the true nature of the word. The New Testament talks about how another prophet will come. First, the Holy Ghost is mentioned, then the Comforter. It is the Prophet Muhammad that fulfills this verse/prophecy. It is Muhammad that feels the Christians' Holy Ghost's (the Angel Gabriel) embrace. He received guidance and the final revelations of God's book (the Quran). Finally, it is Muhammad who is the Comforter that comes as a mercy to mankind and gives the people the true message from God.

Muhammad's mission is very different from Jesus' mission. Muhammad is told in the Quran that he and the small group of believers must fight if Islam (God's religion) is disseminated across the earth. Jesus' mission was not to fight the Hellenistic pagan people or the Roman Empire. The Jews lost two engagements with the Roman Empire and they fought again, but victory was just not meant to be.

Before Muhammad died Islam as a faith was complete from the perspective of God. Islam spread to every corner of Arabia and all the tribal people were content. Muhammad preached to the people in his last sermon that an Arab is not better than a non-Arab and a white is not better than a Black. He affirmed that on the Day of Judgment, all would be judged based on piety. On Muhammad's death bed he told his ten closest followers, to choose among themselves the first Caliphate or ruler. One brother asked, "Ya Muhammad if you had a choice, who would it be?" Muhammad then replied, "Abu Bakr." Ali, the Prophet's cousin, the youngest of the men, was also one of the ten brothers present. The brothers gathered again after the passing and burial of the last Prophet, all except Ali. The brothers chose Abu Bakr as the first Caliphate.

The Shia's story and history of this event were a little different. I am a Sunni Muslim. The Shia people place emphasis on Ali not being present for the vote; however, when Ali did arrive and was told who the Caliphate was he immediately gave allegiance to Abu Bakr. The history behind this event does not say that Ali was insistent on being the Caliphate because he was the cousin of the Prophet, although the Quran says to respect the Prophet's family. Most importantly, history does not say or show that Ali waged a war against Abu Bakr. Another fast is that the second Caliph was Omar. Once again Ali accepted Omar's allegiance and his administration. Islam grew and moved out of Arabia. Omar is credited for conquering the Persian Empire and pushing the Roman Empire out of Jerusalem. On the scarce site where the Temple Solomon was located trash littered the area where Prophet David, Solomon, and Jesus preached. This is where the Quran talks about the farthest Masjid (Al-Aqsa) and where Muhammad ascended to heaven.

> *Glory to (God) Who did take His Servant (Muhammad) for a Journey by night from the Sacred Mosque to the Farthest Mosque, whose precincts*

We did bless in order that We might
show him some of our Signs: for He is
the One Who heareth and seeth (all
things).
[Bani Israel, 17:1][8]

Omar started building the Masjid Aqsa, also known as the Dome of the Rock. Osman became the third Caliphate and again, Ali accepts Osman as a Caliph. History does not mention any arguments and or wars between the two men. Osman was Caliphate for approximately 12 years and Islam spread rapidly throughout Northern Africa, all of the Middle East and Asia. Lastly, Ali became the fourth Caliphate and his administration started with much difficulty. Osman's rule ended with his death while reading the Quran. The social problems from Osman's administration in the city of Medina carried over into Ali's administration. Umayyad, one of the ten brothers that voted for the first three Caliphates who lived in Bagdad did not recognize Ali as Caliphate. Umayyad was upset that Ali did not revenge on the death of his tribal brother Osman. Approximately 100 brothers were willing to travel to Bagdad to help Ali force Umayyad to accept Ali as Caliphate. History states that Ali won this battle with many casualties and Umayyad reluctantly accepted Ali as Caliphate. Ali had three more conflicts before he was killed after four years of being Caliphate. The Islamic faith expanded to Spain in the West and lands past India in the East. Hassan, Ali's son became

---

[8] Quran: chapter 17

the next Caliphate but Umayyad offered 100 dirhams annually for him to be Caliphate and this is how he rose to power. Umayyad was Caliphate for an extended period of time. He is not considered a rightly-guided Caliphate by Sunni Muslim scholars because he made his son Caliph at the time of his death. The people in Medina were in opposition, they wanted Hussein, Ali's second son to be Caliph. Umayyad's son sent a letter to Hussein telling him to come to Bagdad and he would hand over the title to him. Omar's son told Hussein not to go. Due to the people's insistence, Hussein, like his father, traveled to Bagdad with approximately 100 men. Before they made it to Bagdad, they were ambushed and killed. Some say Hussein was buried in Egypt and some say a part of his body is buried in Iraq.

At this time in Islamic history, there is only one Islam and the people are called Muslims. The word Sunni means the tradition of the Prophet and the word Shia means sect. The people in the city of Medina continue to say that Hussein should have been the Caliphate. The Shia movement starts as a political concept but after 300 years it became a damaging sect of the Islamic faith. The Muslims that changed and believed in the Shia ideology did more damage to the faith than the Crusades. Imagine sitting at the dinner table and your son says to you, "Daddy, Ali should have been the first Caliph." What can you do but argue a little and continue to eat with your son who now a rival to the practical aspect of the religion? This period in Islamic history shows how the Caliphs fall short of their Islamic objectives. The Arab men of Arabia were the Caliphs, the generals of the military and the statesmen. Although the people they converted to eventually spoke Arabic and called themselves Arabs they were not the full-blooded Arabs of Arabia. The Arab conquest of the world ended 92 years after the Prophet, whom historians give great respect and honor. They had pure Islamic intentions and spread God's creed that God is solely One and Muhammad is the last Prophet. Many people of the book were well pleased that God sent another Prophet to purify the understanding of religious practice, to clear the concept of what Jesus was and is, and the next coming of Him. Every Muslim in the Islamic world believed in the same simple creed with no heresy and no need for councils. A complete and practical way of life that was spiritually pure leads to heaven but there are challenges on the road to the straight path.

The Shia sect was predominately in Persia. The Persians hated the Arabs with a passion. There were some decisive wars with Arab Sunni dynasties against the Shia Persians but they could not stop the mental sickness of the people. In the first month of the Islamic calendar, the Shia practice a holiday called Ashura, mourning the martyrdom of Hussein Ali's son where the men take a chain and beat themselves over their backs. The Islamic faith has two holidays, the day Ibrahim was to sacrifice his son Ishmael (during the Hajj, Eid-Adha) and the end of Ramadan (Eid-Fitr), the fasting month. The Shia has about five holidays. They continue to mourn the deaths of Ali, Hassan and

Hussein, which is considered a very big sin in this faith. They beat themselves out of punishment because history says only 100 men helped Ali and Hussein in the battles. Perhaps, if they had more men history would be different. You cannot change history or what happened yesterday. The proud Persian people have created this large sect and they now have written books, and educated their children about the madness. Furthermore, they target the Sunni Muslims to convert which caused Sunni Muslims to despise them.

The conquests of these spiritual but tribal and unorganized Arab Muslims were achieved by understanding the goals and objectives of Muhammad and the Islamic faith. Using this, they were able to successfully use their faith as a dominating force. The tribal fighting came back quickly among the Arab people. Political fighting took place over leadership and division was introduced by the Shia sect. Islam continued to expand, Christians converted to the faith that guaranteed them entry into heaven, and the Romans and Byzantine empires lost wars and precious lands. The people had a sense of honor, dignity and a firm understanding of the faith, unlike at the start of Christianity. Muhammad (PBUH) mentioned that a great leader would come out of Turkey; Muslims would be in Italy and take the Christians' strong holds. The early Muslims had an aggressive and successful conversion system for the Christians and pagan people because within fifty to one hundred years after the introduction of Islam, 90% of the people converted. They all believed in the same creed (La ilaha illah, Muhammadur rasul-Allah) there is no god but God and Muhammad is the last Prophet. In Jerusalem, the Muslims did not stop a Christian or a Jew from worshipping and practicing. Nor did they murder them or destroy their places of worship; however, they controlled the state.

The next 300 hundred years are the golden age of Islam. The white Christians did not dominate the Middle East, the Roman Empire was strictly in central Europe and the Persian Empire became Islamic. The ancient Ptolemaic dynasty in Egypt and all of North Africa were Islamic, as well as the ancient Seleucid dynasty in Syria, accompanied by ancient Babylon or Iraq, Turkmenistan, Uzbekistan, Tajikistan, and Afghanistan. Turkey, India, south China and Prussia or Russia experienced Islamic presence by the 10th century. The people across the land were happy. There was an education for children, many small businesses, and a practical covenant and most importantly, all the Muslim people believed in the exact same creed. Most importantly, countries like Syria, Egypt and Iraq, all of which had Christian and Jewish populations continued to remain present in the Islam domain, living in peace and protection under the Sharia laws. However, peace did not last in the city named for peace (Jerusalem). Lastly, the Prophet's companions and successors had remarkably changed one-third of the face of the earth from ignorance and idolatry into the light of knowledge, wisdom, freedom and justice.

It is ironic that the Sunni Muslims acknowledge the

four right-guided Caliphates, but they practice a monarch political government system. The Shia state that there should be a monarch system but they continue to elect their presidents. The Sunni Muslims are politically incorrect and they have practiced an incorrect form of government for approximately 1500 years; not to mention the first 50 years. This is extremely hurting the Muslim people. The Arab monarch government represents their families first and foremost, which is representative of old tribal traditions. Unfortunately, the USA and European countries provide support to these governments with finances and sometimes military assistance.

Chapter V

The Unmerciful Crusader Wars

The perpetuation of White Christian aggression
acts of hatred and violence against other faiths.
How Christian kings, Emperors, Popes and
Crusaders organized world destruction.

It was understood that the Middle-Eastern world
was predominately Islamic. From the seventh to the tenth
century, Muslims dominated the political, economic,
educational and military world stage. Defeated and
outnumbered, Christians were forced to live under Islamic
control. The Abbasid Caliphate ruled the people, provided
many madrasas (schools) for children, and supported a
free and fair marketplace and trading system. Throughout
the Islamic community, the call of prayer was heard in the
streets and throughout the Islamic world, all the Muslim
people believed and practice the same ethics.

In the eleventh century, first, the Egyptians and the
Syrians were fighting over religion (Sunni against Shia);
secondly, the Muslims were starting to lose territory in
Spain, thirdly, the Muslims lost their naval supremacy in
the Mediterranean Sea therefore, they lost the island of
Sardinia and the largest island Sicily. The Crusaders
launched a war based on lies told by Pope Urban II. It is
said that the first crusade consisted of two groups, the
elites (the knights) sailing from England and the peasants
walking. When they both arrived in the Middle East (1095)
they both had a very strong stink on them, the Caliph was

weak and did not have an army, did not understand the reason these warring people came and it was very difficult negotiating with foul smelly people. As a result, the peasants' crusaders defeated the Seljuq Muslims in Turkey and Northern Syria. The siege lasted 9 months and ended on June 1098. The end result was genocide of Muslim civilians' men, women, and children. The knight crusaders captured Tripoli and set it up as an independent principality; next, the crusaders advanced to Jerusalem in June of 1099 the siege lasted for one month after the capture, and the entire Muslim population was put to the sword and decimated in the Masjid Al-Aqsa and the floor was sunken ankle-deep in blood. The Christian crusaders did not spare anyone; people of the Jewish faith were a part of the bloodshed as well. This was the first of many massacres and was conducted by white European Christians.

The Second Crusade (1145-1149) was led by Roman Catholics from Europe. Many belligerent European countries supported the mission of the crusaders by obeying directions from the Papacy. Well-organized and disciplined soldiers arrived in the Middle East in naval fleets. The Muslims were very tribal and crippled by divisions in the faith, weak leadership, and war amongst each other. Although the Christian people that had converted to Islam and the Muslims, in general, understood the faith and came together to fight the aggressive wrongful Christians, one mistake can cause the war and the Seljuq Turks separately defeated both

European kings Louis VII of France and Conrad III of Germany. The Papacy recognized that when Muslims conquered Christian lands, the conquest included the conversion of the inhabitants.

A wise Pope would find out why the Christian people are converting to the Islamic faith instead of starting wars. The Middle East was over 50% Islamic, and Turkey the heart or nucleus of the Byzantine territory empires and or East Roman Empire are converting to Islam too. It is possible that the Seljuq Turks Muslim soldiers were not all born Muslims but converted Christians. Eventually, the Muslims conquered territory in Turkey and most important Damascus with help from Nur-udin Zangi forces. However, the divided but strong Muslims in the Middle East do not help their brethren in Iberia (Spain) therefore, they were decisively defeated in 12th-century battles.

With relentless determination to gain control, the Roman Catholic Church and European Kings led the Third Crusade (1189-1192). The Arab Muslim people tried their best to obey what the Quran prescribed and continued to adhere to Muhammad's teachings, but his vision for the world was underway. Muhammad(Pbuh) informed the Arab Muslims of the need to spread the faith to the people that were not present at his farewell speech. He talked about a great leader that would come out of Turkey and said that the Muslims would conquer the Byzantine Empire. The Muslims lived under the Sharia laws and practiced the ethical laws of warfare pertaining to aggression.

Again the two powers (Egyptians Fatimid's and Syria's Hejaz) in the region were still fighting each other and the first crusade held Jerusalem captured until 1187 when Salahadin retook the city. To do this, Salahadin undertook the difficult task of getting the Egyptians and Syrians to stop fighting each other. He repeated what the Prophet said, "When Muslims fight Muslims they fight over hell and when Muslims fight Christians they fight over heaven." Salahadin put an end to the Fatimid rule in Egypt, defeated the Zangids in Damascus, therefore, became the sole ruler or Sultan of Egypt and Syria. Now the Ayyubids dynasty (Kurdish) under the leadership of Salahadin's march against Jerusalem decimated the Christians to a man, therefore, Jerusalem capitulated in October 1187 and the Christian rule lasted 88 years. Know that the Caliphate in Bagdad had very little say over Jerusalem and absolutely no allegiance to Spain; this was demonstrative of how weak political power and weak military strength caused trouble for the Muslims against the relentless European Christians.

Some Islamic scholars criticize Salahadin greatly. When King Richard, the lion-heart was sick, Salahadin sent his doctor. Salahadin scrutinized the Christian army from a high point and saw disorganization, quarreling and confusion on the part of the crusade forces, therefore, the battle did not start that day. He states he did not want to slaughter the Christian soldiers. Based on different sources some say Salahadin never won a victory over Richard the lionheart and some argue the contrary. However, at the end of the third crusader, the negotiated peace treaty stated the Muslims to retain Jerusalem and worse Salahadin continue to allow the Christian forces and armies to have forts in the coastal areas. Did he forget about the First Crusade when the Christian Knights and peasants slaughtered and massacred thousands of mostly Muslims and some Jews? Salahadin told King Richard if Christian people wanted to enter Jerusalem to pray and trade then the doors would be open but if Christian people want to spill innocent people's blood then the doors will be closed. In spite of hostilities, there was a good deal of exchange of courtesies and manifestation of chivalry on both sides. Even in England's history, Salahadin was a respected Sultan and great statesman.

The Fourth and Fifth Crusades can be viewed as one extended war. In the fourth Crusade (1202-1204), the Christian people were motivated by hatred; they were determined to force their agenda, their beliefs and their domination. Determined to enforce their agenda and dominate, Christians continued to infringe upon the beliefs of Muslims in The Fourth Crusade (1202-1204). The crusade began with disorganization in their attempt to fully conquer and control by defeating the Egyptians. But instead, the Crusades sailed to Constantinople (Turkey) from Venice and sacked, pillaged and plundered the Eastern Orthodox Christians. Constantinople burned for eight days and nights and was reduced to ashes. For several days the extremist Crusaders enacted the worst scenes of destruction, devastation, and outrage also known as the Latin massacre 60,000-80,000 (western Europeans) Eastern Orthodox Christians were put to death by the sword. The Crusaders deposed the Byzantine emperor and put their nominee on the throne. Finally, the Crusaders were Roman Catholics who practiced and believed differently from the Eastern Orthodox churches, furthermore, they could not agree to make one doctrine or one orthodox or one Christianity. Who has the power, who has the great military might and who is more corrupt with hatred, mercilessness and anger in their souls? Well, the answer is, the Roman Empire, its Popes, the Roman Catholic Church, Western Europeans and their kings!

The fourth Crusade, some called the "Curse Crusade," never made it to Egypt or Jerusalem. After the Papacy slaughtered the Greek Orthodox Christians, the Pope wanted to restore the Roman Catholic Church and extend help. The wise the Greek people chose to seek protection from the Seljuq Muslims.

The Fifth Crusade was charged with the views of fanatical and extremist Christian people and the Papacy that indoctrinated people with hatred. Children were urged to take the cross and go to Muslim lands and start a conflict. Insane notions that God would give these innocent children passage through the Mediterranean were upheld by the Papacy, convincing people with the story of the children of Israel who had passed through the Red Sea. This fanciful dream of the invincibility of the innocent children was soon shattered. As the children walked to the east, they were preyed upon by unscrupulous slave traders. No child reached the holy land; most were captured and sold into slavery. Few returned to recount the tale.

During the Sixth Crusade (1213-1221), one must ask where is the brotherhood of Islam. The Christians are starting to fight each other and disagree when it comes to the church and political power. The Christians' aim continued to be the acquisition of Jerusalem and the rest of the Holy Land from Muslim rule. When it came to fighting the Muslims the Christians united together strong, determined and with no mercy on their swords. The belligerence of Crusaders was many European countries and one Muslim enemy state the Seljuq Sultanate of Rum (Persian Shia Muslims) all against one the Ayyubids of Egypt. These Seljuq Turks decisively defeated the Crusaders in the second crusade but now they allied with the crusaders in the Fifth Crusade and attack the Ayyubids in Syria. What kind of Muslims were these people? Where is the Islamic unity, and who is the Caliphate? The weak-minded Muslim leaders (Al-Adil succeeded by Al-Kamil) did not care about the well-being of the Holy land under Islamic rule they only care about Egypt. Al-Kamala did not want to fight the well-organized crusader forces. He was willing to relinquish Jerusalem as long as Egypt was left alone. However, the vengeful crusaders sought retribution for the victories of the Salahadin Ayyubids dynasty. With the fall of Egypt, Jerusalem would automatically be restored under Christian rule. With this motive, Crusaders captured the port city of Damietta and marched down to Cairo. With help from the flooding of the Nile (nature) and rampant disease, the Muslims won the war after a night's attack on the Crusaders. When the Crusaders realized that they were losing the battle they asked for a truce. Terms of peace were negotiated and the sixth Crusade came to an inglorious end for the Christians.

The Seventh Crusade (1228-1239) was full of organized iniquity. This was not a good century for the Islamic world. Muslim leaders lacked dignity and demonstrated irresponsibility and disrespect. The Christians had complete confidence in their diplomatic maneuvers, their military domination, and their support from the kings and commanders of European countries. Although the Papacy wanted to spill more Islamic blood, Fredrick II negotiated with Al-Kamil to secede Jerusalem and surrounding territories to Christian rule. Other empires were starting wars in the Far East, implicating the future of the Muslim people. Genghis Khan, the emperor of the Mongol Empire entered the world stage as a veritable tyrant. Under his direction, the Mongolian army reduced populous cities to rubble, destroyed centuries of culture, and massacred millions of people from central Asia, China, the Middle East and Europe. Having dominated and forced many countries to submit to the Mongolian empire, Halaka, a grandson of Genghis Khan was commissioned to conquer Persia and Iraq. Halaka asked the Khwarezmian Empire to open a trade route through their country (Iran) and they reluctantly did so with much resentment. He then asked the Abbasid Caliph in Bagdad to send a contingent against the Assassins, but he ignored the letter. The Caliphate wanted the Shah or ruler of the Khwarezmian to recognize and give allegiance to the Caliphate. Like most Muslim countries, the Shah refused and gave no respect to the Abbasid Caliph. Caliph was elated after the Mongols attacked the Khawarzam Shah which signified an end to a long-standing rival. The Mongols also assaulted the strongholds of the Assassins who had let loose a reign of terror for other Muslims. Turkmenistan, Uzbekistan, and Iran countries were invaded and destroyed with extreme massacres. The Khwarezmids, a fierce, uncivilized race, were driven from their country. Settling in Palestine, they were unable to forget the rage that expelled them from their land. Riots, murder and destruction accompanied the Khwarezmids upon their entry into Palestine, determined to cleanse Palestine of the Christian faith. The insolence these people promoted caused the Christian and Muslim truce to be broken. The Syrians and the Egyptians unified against the barbaric conduct of their neighbor and sought to restore Palestine.

Unfortunately, the Muslims of Spain were immersed in the hateful Christian world. The Moors never gave allegiance to any Caliphs in Bagdad; therefore, the Caliphs never sent any army to Spain for aid. The Al-Mohads of Morocco, the Marinids of Morocco and the Zayanids of Algerians were continually fighting each other for domination of the area; the winner would go into Spain to also dominate the Muslims there. "When Muslims fighting Muslims they fight over the fire this makes the Muslims very weak and vulnerable, therefore, easy victories for the Christians." The Muslim rule in Spain was practically over by 1258. The Muslims had not learned anything from history and even whatever little of Spain was left to them they made no effort to unite and face the enemy as a solid front.

In Bagdad, the Mongols attacked the heartland of Islam, the Abbasid Caliph was trampled under the hoofs of the Mongol's horse, and the people were slaughtered and a massacre history recorded over 2 million people. The saddest event in the history of Islam, put blame on the Abbasid Caliph, he was critiqued by other Islamic states and Sultans, the consensus being that he was a failed political figurehead, a commander without a military, and an incompetent Islamic leader. Furthermore, he did not give leadership, good advice or stop Muslims from fighting Muslims and worse could not help the Muslims in the Holy Land, the Muslims in surrounding areas, and the Muslims in Spain from the onslaught of the merciless Christian Popes, Kings and the Crusaders and also the Mongols. As the result of this Crusade, the Muslims lost all the territory and respected that Salahadin had won. In the Muslim world, the restoration of Jerusalem to the Christians without a fight sent a wave of anger against Al-Kamil of Egypt.

The Muslims patiently waited for these peace treaties to end before they began a new siege. In 1245 As-

Salih Ayyub laid siege to Jerusalem. The city fell to the Muslims once again after a short siege. That triggered the eighth crusade (1248-1254) led by Louis IX of France with approximately 800,000 troops entering Egypt where they were captured and decisively defeated by Ayyubid Sultan Turanshah supported by the Bahariyya Mamluks. Perhaps, because it was so easy to defeat the Moors in Spain the European kings thought the same for the Middle East Muslims. The Mongols continued to advance to Palestine where they met the Mamluk of Egypt and were defeated in 1260 at the Battle of Ain Jalut by Qutuz and his General Baibars. As Sultan, confident Baibars proceeded to attack the Christian Crusaders' stronghold of Arsuf, Athlith, Haifa, Safad, Jaffa, Ascalon and Caesarea and the Crusader fortress cities fell systematically.

White Christian domination still has not come to an end as we embark on the Eighth and Ninth Crusade. The eighth crusade started in 1270 in Tunisia, the belligerent Kingdom of France and Anjou against the Hafsids. Hafsids were Berber Sunni Muslims, their territories stretched from Algeria to Libya. Again the Crusaders decided the city of Damietta; Egypt should be the focus of the attack. If crusaders controlled Damietta, then the Nile River they could easily attack Palestine and recapture Jerusalem. King Louis IX of France was captured and defeated and was forced to give up the city. In the ninth crusade 1271-1272 the belligerent the Mongols and always many Christian countries against one, the Mamluks of the Bahris dynasty victory, this was the end of the Crusaders in the Middle

East, the end of the Kingdom of Jerusalem, and the imminent collapse of the last remaining strongholds along the Mediterranean coast (Acre and Ruad Island). All conflict started in the Levant territorial between Syria and Egypt and all conflict ended when these two countries resolved their problems.

When Syria and Egypt united, they were able to defeat foreign evil aggression, such as the Mongols in the battle of Shaqhab in 1303. After 208 years of wars that were instigated by the mendacious Roman Catholic Papacy, the genocide of innocent Muslims occurred in the fall of Ruad. Mamluk soldiers defeated and forced the armored Knights and bowmen to surrender and imprisoned them in Cairo. Surely, if the tables were turned the Muslims sailing to England to start wars and strictly kill Christians, the Christian army would have decimated these Muslims without remorse. Similarly, the American British Christian military forces wage war today and take no prisoners and like crusaders, they murder and kill their enemies without any sign of mercy.

Known as the Capitulation of Granada, the treaty provided a temporary truce, followed by the relinquishment of the sovereign Moorish Emirate of Granada in January 1492 (founded five centuries earlier) to the Catholic monarchs of Spain. The treaty guaranteed a set of rights to the Moors, including religious tolerance and fair treatment in return for their surrender and capitulation. The treaty revoked some protections provided to Granada's Muslims and Jews.

The capitulation of 1492 contained sixty-seven articles among which were the following:

- That both great and small should be perfectly secure in their persons, families, and properties.
- That they should be allowed to continue in their dwellings and residences, whether in the city, the suburbs, or any other part of the country.
- That their laws should be preserved as they were before, and that no one should judge them except by those same laws.
- That their mosques, and the religious endowments appertaining to them, should remain as they were in the times of Islam.
- That no Christian should enter the house of a Muslim, or insult him in any way.
- That no Christian or Jew holding public offices by the appointment of the late Sultan should be allowed to exercise his functions or rule over them.
- That all Muslim captives taken during the siege of Granada, from whatever part of the country they might have come, but especially the nobles and chiefs mentioned in the agreement, should be liberated.
- Such Muslim captives as might have escaped from their Christian masters, and taken refuge in Granada, should not be surrendered; but the Sultan should be bound to pay the price of such captives to their owners.
- That all those who might choose to cross over to Africa should be allowed to take their departure within a certain time, and be conveyed thither in the king's ships, and without any pecuniary tax

being imposed on them, beyond the mere charge for passage, and

- That after the expiration of that time no Muslim should be hindered from departing, provided he paid, in addition to the price of his passage, the tithe of whatever property he might carry along with him.
- That no one should be prosecuted and punished for the crime of another man.
- That the Christians who had embraced Islam should not be compelled to relinquish it and adopt their former creed.
- That any Muslim wishing to become a Christian should be allowed some days to consider the step he was about to take; after which he is to be questioned by both a Muslim and a Christian judge concerning his intended change, and if, after this examination, he still refused to return to Islam, he should be permitted to follow his own inclination.
- That no Muslim should be prosecuted for the death of a Christian slain during the siege; and that no restitution of property taken during this war should be enforced.
- That no Muslim should be subject to have Christian soldiers billeted upon him, or be transported to provinces of this kingdom against his will.
- That no increase should be made to the usual imposts, but that, on the contrary, all the oppressive taxes lately imposed should be immediately suppressed.
- That no Christian should be allowed to peep over the wall or into the house of a Muslim or enter a mosque.

- That any Muslim choosing to travel or reside among the Christians should be perfectly secure in his person and property.
- That no badge or distinctive mark be put upon them, as was done before.
- That no should be interrupted in the act of calling the people to prayer, and no Muslim molested either in the performance of his daily devotions or in the observance of his fast, or in any other religious ceremony; but that if a Christian should be found laughing at them he should be punished for it.
- That the Muslims should be exempted from all taxation for a certain number of years.
- That the Lord of Rome, the Pope, should be requested to give his assent to the above conditions and sign the treaty himself.[9]

The Christians did not keep their word and before the end of the 15th century, the large population of Muslims and Jews was deported from now Roman Catholic Spain. To end this 500-year period in history, it is said the greatest civilization in history was the Moors in Spain. They established universities for scholarly work, free trade, good commerce, and technological and scientific innovations. They must be noted for the successful integration of Jews, Muslims and Christians who lived together in harmony and the ethnic tolerance that was practiced by many different ethnic groups (Arabs, Berbers, Africans and Europeans) under their rule. It is unfortunate

---

[9] Internet: Wikipedia.org

that the Moor's adversaries from the northern countries of France, Germany, and England could not learn from the civility of the Moors.

To end this chapter in history, there were no Jews and Muslims in Western Europe at the end of the 15th century. The white Christians truly showed their dominance through mercilessness, intolerance, and unremorseful behavior. They may write their history with glory, but if no mercy is shown to God's creatures, then He will give no mercy on the Day of Judgment.

In the Middle East after the end of the Crusader's wars, the Muslim people and or the Sultans did not destroy Christian churches and or kill Christian civilian people. In Jerusalem the church of the sepulcher was there for service, the Jewish people were free to worship, trade and travel both groups were free to practice their individual faith under Islamic law and have protection. Also, there were Jews and Christians throughout the Islamic world, in Iraq, Iran, Egypt, Syria and Turkey all free to worship, to trade, get an education and most important was not forced to convert. As an organization, the Papacy sought to attain absolute domination over the world. The Papacy, European Kings and the Crusader's souls' are marred with blood. The omniscient and omnipotent God of Ibrahim will give these people their due on the Day of Judgment.

Chapter VI

The Domination Period
The subordinates of the church
White European world assault
on non-whites of the world
1500 to 1865

The Renaissance that occurred in Florence, Italy, from 1350 to 1650, coincided with the rejection of Christianity by the leading intellectuals of Europe. Stimulated by nostalgia for ancient Greece and Rome, defined the Renaissance was the revival and renewal of paganism. This revival of idol worship caused Western Civilization to revert to its original theme, continuing its development ever since accordingly. Nicolo Machiavelli is one of the dominant personalities of The Renaissance. He epitomized the spirit of this period through the promotion of nationalist and patriotic ideals. As a father of the modern totalitarian form of governance, he dreamt of unifying Italy as a dominant world power. The availability of paper and the invention of type speed allowed for the dissemination of ideas, thought, and reason. After the Protestant Reformation, the scholars of the renaissance discovered the most powerful of all weapons in their arsenal against the Christian church-science! The government began to control the many separate Protestant churches everywhere in Europe. Like always, the spiritual power of religion became subordinate to the interests of secular politics.

The development of secularism in the European

intelligentsia, from the Renaissance onward, was a violent reaction to the atrocities committed in the name of the church in its futile mission to suppress heresy. The Protestants were no less superstitious and cruel than the Catholics. Both leaders of the protestant reformation Martin Luther and John Calvin were firm believers in witchcraft mania. In the light of these appalling historical facts, it was only inevitable that more and more intense hatred and rebellion against the clergy was kindled in the hearts of the people and the leading intellectuals condemned the church and the analogy, all religions, as superstition and fanaticism, thus secularism was equated with "enlightenment." In the age of enlightenment, the goal was to reform society using reason (rather than tradition, faith and revelation) and advance knowledge through science. Science and intellectual exchange were favored as opposed to superstition, intolerance and abuses made by the church and state.

After the destruction of the church's power and authority, a lesser evil was replaced with a great one. The Europeans regarded themselves as absolutely free to act as their reason and circumstances dictated and feeling accountable to nothing and nobody, a western man set out with extraordinary energy, organization and technology to bring the enticing world under their domination. Now with the coming of the "Age of exploration" from 1500 to the 17th century, western historians have more accurate label this period as the "Age of Imperialism." The atrocities and genocides committed by these European criminals had no parallel in past history or previous civilizations. Unscrupulousness was the rule with greed for riches and lust for power knowing no limits.

The British lifestyle was bleak in the 1800s. There were enough criminals within the empire to ship them off to colonies where they contaminated the natives with the disease. The natives in the Americas, the Aboriginal people of Australia and other indigenous populations started to decline as soon as the Europeans set foot on the land.

For five hundred years, between the 15th and 20th centuries, the entire world was plundered for the benefit of the west and or Christian people. It is an irony that the age of liberal democracy was also the age of imperialism. When Paris was ringing with the revolutionary slogans of liberty, fraternity and equality, the French forces were crushing the independent states of Africa and South-East Asia and were harnessing them under their imperialistic yoke. While democracy reigned supreme in England America, China and India were subjugated and enslaved. These countries were ruthlessly bound to the discretion of European imperialism and vulnerable cultures were inhumanely destroyed.

The Indian industries were strangled to death only to give a lease of life to the Lancashire textile industry. China was impoverished only to enrich Britain. The great shanghai library was burned to ashes only to quench the imperialist thirst for domination. Russia was invaded by western armies from 1610 to 1941. The people of Africa and Asia were subjected to successive waves of imperialist aggression in the form of western missionaries, traders and adventures ever since the 15th century. During this same period, the British colonized America, Australia, New Zealand, and south and east Africa and exterminated or subjugated the Native Americans and the Aborigines. Millions of Africans were enslaved and deported across the Atlantic Ocean in order to serve the European colonizers of the Americas as living tools to minister to their western masters' greed for wealth. Throughout Asia and Africa, every endeavor has been made to eliminate the local cultures. In the minds of the new generation seeds of revolt against their own citizens have been meticulously sowed and through the agency of education and the mass media, an assassination of their minds and thoughts has been accomplished. Their culture and civilization are not tolerated and the system of westernization has been superimposed upon them.[10]

Christian morals and ethics are supposed to be derived from the Ten Commandments. In the New Testament, Jesus says, "Turn the other cheek and love your enemies." This is an extremely difficult practice for Christians. White Christians conduct themselves as if they have not read or heard the Sermon on the Mount or the Sermon on the Plain. These sermons are treated as biblical tales, but Christian people should put them in their hearts, and make them morals, ethics and customs of everyday life. The principles of Muhammad's last sermon were employed by the early Muslims. Christian people only practice one percent of the bible and the remainder of the

---

[10] ibid

book is not a concern. Jesus taught love and grace but the Christian people and their actions show hatred, violence and ethnic intolerance.

The Spanish and Portugal inquisition to force Roman Catholicism on the defeated Jews and most Muslims this regulation of the faith of the newly converted was intensified after the royal decrees issued in 1492 and 1501 ordering Jews and Muslims to convert or leave. There were absolutely no freedoms of religion in all of white Christian Europe or in the cruel Holy Roman Empire. This was not the case in Jerusalem where Muslim leaders lived with Jews and Christians who are even recognized in the Quran.

Next, the expulsion of 300,000 Jews and Muslims from Spain resulted of the dissembling of Ferdinand and Isabella. The Portuguese, Spanish, French and the horrific Brits continued to encounter their long-standing adversary: Arab Muslims. The second generation of Arab Muslims sailed the seas in small boats and docked in South and Southeast Asia and the Pacific (Burma, Malaysia, Indonesia and the Philippines) with the intention of establishing trade, not conversion. These Hindu and Buddhist people saw the sincerity of these Arab Muslims, which was an influential factor that led to natives converting to the Islamic faith. However, in the 15th 16th and 17th centuries, Christianity was not in sub-Sahara Africa, South Africa, or East Africa; nor was there a Christian presence in Asia (India) and Asia-minor. The early white Christian missionaries predominately traveled to

Europe only. The superior weaponry that the Europeans had was a severe advantage. Africans and Asians were still using objects like the sword, the spear and bow and arrow. When armed European explorers saw that the Muslims ruled without oppression or force, the Christians did not hesitate to start wars. The Roman Empire, Roman Catholic Crusader Christians, and the Protestant Christians did not fear God in this age of enlightenment, secularism and imperialism eras.

The Portuguese had a 200-year head start on the export of slaves from Africa before the British, French and Spanish got into the market of human capital. It is estimated that during the 4½ century of the trans- Atlantic slave trade, Portugal was responsible for transporting over 4.5 million Africans (roughly 40% of the total). The Portuguese were the first to engage in the New World slave trade, and other European countries soon followed. Slaves were considered cargo to be transported to the Americas as quickly and cheaply as possible. Once in America, they were to be sold to labor in coffee, tobacco, cocoa, cotton and sugar plantations. They were to mine gold and silver, pick rice in fields, constructing industry, cut timber for ships, and serve whites as domestic servants. The Atlantic slave traders, ordered by trade volume, were: the Portuguese, the British, the French, the Spanish, the Dutch, and the Americans. Outposts were established on the African coast where slaves were purchased from local African tribal leaders. Current estimates convey that roughly 12 million Africans were shipped across the

Atlantic, and the actual number of Africans purchased by the traders is considerably higher. It is also written that not one African that left the shores of Africa was a Christian; remarkably, 20% were Muslims.

The tribal people of sub-Sahara Africa lived with a just political system, and economic system and they were happy under the influence of the Muslims. The indigenous Africans had an understanding that the concept of slavery was a dominant economic tool. The Muslim dynasties constantly fought each other which made them resent each other. It was very easy for the organized white man to come into Africa and make his conquest through unequivocal exploitation. Again the Muslim people were never politically strong; their military was no match against a force that had guns and canons. The indigenous African people did not have the education, aggression, or arrogance needed to combat or defend themselves; therefore, most indigenous Africans were murdered, and after submission, they were enslaved. Territories were rapidly seized and Africa became Europe's game of monopoly.

What gave these Europeans the audacity to come to Africa with their imperialistic goals of conquest and colonization? The European imperialist push into Africa was motivated by three main factors: economics, politics, and domination. These white European people are so organized "The Berlin Conference" to control the domination of Africa through the regulation of an Afro-Euro trade system. With this African autonomy and self-government were lost. Africa was then divided between Britain, France, Belgium, Spain, Portugal, Italy and Germany. Lines were drawn on a map of places Europeans had never been to, without regard for existing kingdoms, geography or the people living there. Europeans believed that they were bringing civilization to 'savage people', liberating Africa from Arab slave traders. Christianity was introduced, as well as new forms of trade, education, labor and judiciary systems. Once it was discovered that Africa had mineral and agricultural wealth, the Europeans were keen to exploit the natural resources of the land as well.

The primary motivation for European intrusion was economic capital greed, also known as capitalism. Many African states and rulers such as the Ashanti, the Ethiopians, the Moroccans, Somalia's, the Benin Empire and the Zulus resisted the wave of European aggression. However, the industrial revolution had provided the Europeans with advanced weapons such as machine guns, which African armies found difficult to resist with the exception of the Ethiopians and Liberians who remained free from the colonization.

New technology, new inventions, and changes in agriculture and manufacturing had a profound effect on the social, economic and cultural condition of Great Britain. Is this a God-given of resource and information for humanities or is this because of England's intelligence, researchers, sciences and discoveries? British Industrial Revolution subsequently spread throughout Western Europe, North America, Japan and slowly the rest of the world. The question is should the resources and energy be for the betterment of humanity or for its destruction? Because of the nature of these European Christian people, the latter is the answer.

The British managed to lead conquests on five different fronts: the Americas, the continent of Africa, East India, Southeast Asia and Australia. The cruelest and most manipulative group of white Christians was the British Empire. Complete domination over their colonies' sovereignty gave the British Empire supreme authority over the territory and the autonomy to dictate the law. One example, in a single day's battle for Sudan, 10,800 Sudanese killed compared with 48 British soldiers. The British not unlike the other European countries had conquered part of America, Africa, India, south-east Asia and Australia as well as fighting now the Ottoman Empire.

The fall of Constantinople and or the Byzantine Empire in 1453 under the command of 21-year old Ottoman Sultan Mehmed II, in 1492 the end of the Muslim rule in Spain, Bayezid II, and the sultan of the Ottoman Empire sent out the Ottoman Navy to Spain to evacuate the Jews safely to the Middle East. He ridiculed the conduct of Ferdinand II of Aragon and Isabella I of Castile in expelling a class of people (Muslims and Jews) so useful to their society. Next, the rise of the Ottoman Empire the conquest of the entire Mamluk Sultanate of Egypt, Syria, Iraq, and Arabia with the heart of the Arab world now under their control Selim I, the son of Bayezid II took the title of Caliph of Islam, being the first Ottoman Sultan to do so. This was completely the end of Arabs being the Caliph's and Sultans. Within the next century, the Ottoman Empire expanded with victories in southern Europe but the Ottoman had one big adversary in the Muslim world, the Persian Shia remained a separate, rival and for the most part a hostile state. The greatest enemy to the Islamic faith and the Muslim people throughout history will always be the Shia Muslims of Persia present-day Iran. The Shia of Persia helped Genghis Khan and were spared the bloodshed. In the 16th and 17th centuries, they were trained in the rules and customs of the English militia and helped the Christendom for the purpose of uniting them in a confederacy against the Ottoman Empire. Between 1602 and 1612 and again between 1616 and 1627, Persia and Turkey were at war and the Persians won a number of successes. Distracted by this struggle in the east, the Turks were starting to lose battles in Europe signing treaties now dictated by the Europeans. The Christendom's skills in weaponry and warfare on land became equal if not superior, however, at the sea, the infidels were far supreme. By the end of the sixteenth century, the Muslims in the Horn of Africa, Egypt, southeast Africa, and Southeast Asia were all crying for help "where was the Caliph, and his army to fight the Christian Portuguese and next comes the British.

One of the first Tsar of Russia (1533) was in the company of a Muslim Imam and a Christian Priest and he ask both one question, "In what religion can I drink Vodka?" Immediately the Priest responded, "In the

Christian faith men can drink vodka in fact the people can drink wine and any intoxicating drink." The Tsar looked at the Imam, "Muslims cannot drink any intoxicating beverage because we believers cannot pray intoxicated," therefore, the Tsar stated, "I will become a Christian because I like drinking vodka. It was possible this Tsar was Ivan the terrible, he accepted the Eastern Orthodox Church and or present-day Russia Orthodox his long reign saw the conquest of the Khanates of Kazan (the Golden Horde), Astrakhan and Siberia all Islamic states and mostly Muslim population from 1552 to 1568 wars with these three Muslim states, much of the Muslim population massacred, the Tsar celebrated his victory by building several churches. However, Russia becomes a multi-ethnic and multi-faith state spanning almost one billion acres.

The discovery and exploitation of the new world for the first time provided Christian Europeans with ample supplies of gold and silver. The fertile lands of the new colonies, along with European presence in Africa, and South and Southeast Asia, accelerated and expanded the Christians' wealth. They were able to grow crops, create trade routes, establish eastern trading companies, and manage cheap labor, and import and export tea, coffee and sugar. On the other hand, Muslims had not changed socially, politically, or economically. They continued to fight and dominate each other, particularly in Nigeria, Mali, and Morocco against Algeria and the Ottoman Empire fighting both Egypt and Persia. Furthermore, the Ottoman Empire suffered serious territorial losses on two fronts: the Russians in the North and the Europeans in the West. Change is needed but change is difficult. In the Ottoman Empire maybe they are too religious, need to abandon old concepts in fighting, old ways of dealing with the outside world, learn new science of diplomacy, and negotiation, and retrain the military to the new weaponry, tactics and strategy.

There were words; call just, ethical, compassionate, sympathetic and right or good behavior. The white Christians have none of these words on their tongue or in their soul. They do have mass slaughter-massacres-rape torture of non-whites and nor-Christians people; full of aggression, anger and destruction of property, farmlands, villages, and livestock absolutely nothing is spared. Their European industrial revolution gave these white creatures a weapon of mass destruction and they went straight down to the black continent to practice their military strategies against these peaceful people. White Christians are not people of God, they have no fear of God in their souls, they work for the devil; they believe they are the supreme race, they are better than all the nor-white people; they believe they have the right to mass murder any race of people, to change laws and customs that people should follow their lead and worship their many man-made religions, denominations and finally join them in hell in the next life. All equals the "white man's burden," that they are responsible to govern and the full cultural impact of everyday life. This is purely Christian domination and when will it end?

In conclusion from the 15th century to the end of colonization was an extremely humiliating time for non-white people and non-Christian people. Approximately 10 million to 50 million innocent people lose their lives from the superior weaponry of the cruel white European Christian more than the ancient Roman Empire and the Holy Roman Empire combined. The devil is surely winning the war on earth and it dominates. These European power planned to dominate the world and they did but were the world better? The God of Ibrahim is a merciful and forgiving but also a punishing God the millions of people enslaved, the millions murdered, millions tortured and beaten, brainwash reeducation to Christianization by acculturation, do they want justice. To convert to white Christianity, to be westernized and secularized is to accept all the destructive crimes the European afflicted on the non-Christian and non-white people of the world. Again if the people accepted Christianity and their new cultures then they have forgiven the white man and further there is no need for God to punish the white man. If you talk with an Africa Christian from maybe Nigeria he would tell you it was good that the European Christian came and change the society and culture for the better. However, if you talk with a Muslim Nigerian he would say the opposite, we had a good culture, economic system and communications. At the end of the day mostly everybody in Africa and Asia knows a European language, they understand white Christian capitalism, and worse they have churches and Christian in their population. Once the indigenous now a

Christian has lost all his culture, he may look African but his brain is white, he thinks white, behaves white the complete socialization and psychology of the Africa Christian were based on the European brainwashing of this black man. The same in Asia once Hindus and Buddhists were now Christian the changing of culture equals the changing of behavior the destruction of the person and worse the soul. At the beginning of the 19th century Africa and Asia are still under colonization of white Christian domination when will it end?

For the whole of the 18th century, the Ottoman Empire lost battles after battles on all fronts, losing territories and all respect. The relative weakness of the major Islamic powers has been manifest, small countries like Portugal and Netherlands were able to establish themselves on land in east Africa and at seas in the south Pacific in defiance of the Muslim powers. In 1798 a young general Napoleon Bonaparte invaded, occupied and governs Egypt; the lesson was harsh and clear even a small European force could invade one of the heartlands of the Islamic empire and do so with impunity. The second disgrace was the British Royal Navy, not the Turkish suzerains could get the French out of Egypt. The Christian people of east Europe one by one freed themselves from Ottoman rule and had recognition as an autonomous principality under Ottoman suzerainty. On the other hand the Muslim people of eastern European and or the white Muslim people former Ottoman Empire where Muslims formed the majority or started to form the majority, were mostly expelled, depopulated, assimilated/Christianized, massacred, and ethnic cleans or fled elsewhere all which continues to this day. And the Arab Muslims have no political power, no military power, the Turkish Caliph is a disgrace to the whole Islamic world, and the Christians continue to dominate and advance. The begrudgingly, Arab Muslims would have to reluctantly ask for help from the very people who caused the most trauma to the faith.

In this world, it often happens that violent, crafty and unprincipled seize the desirable goods of this world while the pious go away empty. Dark, unfeeling and unloving powers determine human destiny; the concept of Divine justice, which according to religion rules the world, seems to have no existence. The essence of life in society today can be an aimless, restless activity, and an utterly irrational force. Since the basis of all desire was need, deficiency and thus violence, the nature of brute and man alike is originally and its very essence subject to anger, jealousy, gluttony and more violence, therefore, the white race falls under the prophecy of the people of Gog and Magog, who will terrorize and deceive the nations of the world in all four corners of the earth. Sounds like the Europeans and their cousins white Americans.

Chapter VII

The Church the Bible Christianities
and the many Denominations

Churches Doctrine	Founders	Country	Year	
Roman Catholic	Constantine I	Rome	325 AD	Trinity
Oriental church	Saint Mark	Middle East	4th century	trinity
Eastern church		Middle East	4th century	trinity
Assyrian church	Saint Thomas	Middle East	5thc	Nestorian

These are considered the four early Christian orthodoxies but they all make a very weak claim of succession from the apostles. They state that the bishops succeed one another in succession spreading the gospel of Jesus. These men or Bishops spread different doctrines and dogmas to the ignorant pagan people of that time. Early Christianity had no fixed official doctrine, it had no fixed official belief, what it did have was a whole range of competing and different factions of groups calling themselves Christians, each with their own central doctrine. The fact, when Constantine I chose to become Christian in 325 AD there were many types of Christianities, dogma, doctrines and beliefs of Christianities in the people's minds. No two people in the whole of early Christianity or the Roman Empire believed the same. These four so-called orthodox have absolutely no apostle's succession because neither church was around during the first hundred years of Christianity.

94

These four churches all started after the council of Nicaea in the 4th century and accepted the end doctrine of the trinity. The Jewish-Christian groups were the real apostle's succession people of early Christianity. However, all of the Jewish-Christians groups were destroyed, persecuted, feed to the lions, ethnic cleansed, murdered, from the earth by Roman Emperors, also by these four so-called orthodoxies and their heresy practices. Not one of the first four orthodoxies mentions the participation and the role Jewish groups and sects played in Christianity.

Although the Quran supports the person, Jesus Christ and his 12 apostles by recognizing them as Muslims, Paul destroyed this religious preaching and writing by saying that Jesus is a god, the God, or the son of God. There is no verse in the Bible that supports the trinity, Jesus' divinity or duality in relation to God. This is why the new ruler of Christianity, Constantine started the first Ecumenical council. The Oriental Church and the Anglican Church followed the Roman Catholic Bishops and accepted the trinity. Therefore, they did not have a firm understanding of their own beliefs. Once again the bible does not give certainty on what Jesus is, who he was and what he stood for. Many gospels were destroyed by the Roman Emperors at this time. There were probably more than 100 gospels about Jesus' life. The four gospels that are in most bibles are weak, full of contradictions and plagiarism. Furthermore, the Roman Empire now the Roman Catholic Church, had sovereignty, military power and brute force that coerced the people to submit to their doctrines and beliefs. White Christian domination is here.

Churches Doctrine	Founders	Country		Year	
Protestants	Martin Luther	Germany	1522		trinity
Anglican Church	King Henry VIII	England	1534		trinity
Baptists	John Smith	Amsterdam	1606		trinity
Presbyterians	John Calvin	Scotland	1707		trinity
Lutherans	Martin Luther	Scandinavia	16thc.		trinity
Evangelism	Albert B. Simpson	USA	1887		trinity
Congregational	Robert Browne	Holland	1582		trinity
Puritans	Marian Exiles	England	1558		trinity
Methodists	John Wesley	England	1774		trinity
Pietism	Philipp Jakob Spener	Germane	17th		trinity
Adventists	William Miller	USA	18th		trinity
Pentecostal	Charles Parhan	USA	20th		trinity
Episcopal	Samuel Seabury	New York	18th		trinity
Disciples of Christ	Barton W. Stone	USA	19th		trinity
Holiness	Phoebe Palmer	USA	1840		trinity
Unitarianism	Theophilus Lindley	London	1774		monotheism
Anabaptists	Peter Chelcicky	Czech Republic	15th		trinity
Amish	Jakob Ammann	Switzerland	1693		trinity
Mennonites	Menno Simons	Germane	15th		trinity
Church of England	King Henry VIII	England	16th		trinity
Moravian	Jan Hus	England	14th		trinity
Quakers	George Fox	England	17th		Nontrinitarian

Jehovah's Witness Charles Taze Rusell USA		1879	Nontrinitarian
Mormons	Joseph Smith	USA	1820s	Nontrinitarian
Christian Scientists	Mary Baker Eddy	USA	1879	
7th day Adventist	Joseph Bates	USA	1863	trinity
AME	Richard Allen	USA	1816	trinity

Protestantism grew into many denominations after Martin Luther's publication of the 99 Thesis in the 16th Century. On the NPR radio show, it was said, "If Martin Luther could come back to life to see the results of his 99 Thesis or the results of his protest of the Catholic Church; he would not like the end results. Blame is attributed to the King James Version of the Bible. Protestant sects have a few commonalities: there is absolutely no apostolic succession, their foundation is the Catholic church, the trinity and the first ecumenical council, each denomination is founded by a white man and they all started in England and Germany, not anywhere near Jesus' birthplace, Jerusalem.

Who are Christian people following, personalities? There are three questions God will ask each soul on the Day of Judgment: Who is your Lord? Who is your leader? What religion are you? The whole of the Christian world will answer that Jesus is their Lord. They will wrongfully claim the founders of their denomination as their leaders. The names of their denomination or the names of their churches will be identified as being their religion. The right answer to all of these questions would be known if they had obeyed the Prophets. If God asked Ibrahim to state who his Lord is, Ibrahim would answer, "You are my

Lord, Oh God." If the followers of Ibrahim were asked by God who they followed, they would reply, "We follow Ibrahim." Moses' people would say, "We follow Moses." Jesus' people would say, "We follow Jesus." Surely Muhammad's people would say, "We follow Muhammad." The answer to the final question is written in the Quran, which states, "Don't die but as a Muslim (in a state of Islam)!"

The biggest lie in the history of mankind spoken every Sunday by Priests, Preachers, Ministers, Reverends, Popes and the like, is that the Bible is the word of God. It is a lie used to control the people. Christianity is based on incorrect information and it is a lie to encourage people to rely on blind faith instead of doing necessary historical research. Research says that Paul wrote one-third of the New Testament and we all can say that Paul is a man. When these Christian leaders say that God wrote the Bible does this include Jesus and the Holy Ghost? History says that Jesus did not write the Bible, particularly the New Testament, while the bible states that God and Jesus are the same entity. The book of Mathews recognizes Jesus as a Prophet. By the end of the bible, Jesus is a prophet, a god and the Holy Ghost.

In 1661 King James wrote his version of the Bible. In the preface, he cites the Catholic Bible, Jerusalem Bible and the Greek Bible as sources, all of which contained errors and he is the person who was responsible for fixing them. What new references, sources, facts and information did he use? Please do not say inspired by God.

King James wrote the Protestant bible based on what Martin Luther said, and he based the changes on the actions of the English and German people. Isn't apparent that King James is not God? The King James Bible is five or more books less-than the Catholic Bible. King James and his staff not only changed the grammar and the subject but the entire scriptural text was modified. Confusion is the end result of this book, many different understandings created many denominations. King James was born a Catholic but became a Protestant when his people of England converted from Catholicism during the Protestant protest movement. However, after writing the Protestant Bible and seeing the results or the mess he created he converted back to the Catholic Church. King James realized that after particular men read his version of the bible, new divisions, sects and denominations were founded. This was not good for Christianity. Within the next hundred years, Europe had well over a hundred Protestant denominations.

In retrospect, a hundred years before there were pro-protestant Kings and Queens of England, there was a Queen called "Bloody Mary," or Queen Mary I, the daughter of King Henry VIII (1555). During her reign, she had more than 300 Protestants burned at the stake for heresy. She viewed the Protestant movement as a falsification of the Christian faith and she chiefly supported the Papacy of the Roman Catholic Church. However, she failed to gain the support of the nobles and most of her countrymen to ethnically cleanse the new Protestant faith from Great Britain and Germany.

The Quran says God gave Jesus a book called, "The Injil" which is the original Gospel of Jesus that contains laws, practices, the pure gospel and scripture. The Islamic scholars say that the present four gospels Mathew, Mark, Luke and John are not considered the Injil but fragments of Jesus' message. This tainted verse and distorted scripture changed the meaning of the original teaching that has been forever corrupted:

> "And We sent in their footsteps Jesus, son of Mary, authenticating
> what was present with him of the Torah. And We gave him the Gospel,
> in it was a guidance and a light, and authenticating what was present
> with him of the Torah, and a guidance and a lesson for the righteous." (Quran)[11]

Furthermore in the Quran, God tells Muhammad(Pbuh), "That He is not going to let Muhammad's community (the Muslims and or the Arabs people) destroy this book like the formal two Prophets Moses and Jesus people destroy their books." So when Muhammad received the Quran piece by piece over 23 years from the Archangel Gabriel, he memorized all of the verses as well as his followers, companions, children in schools the whole Islamic world. This dissemination of information was easy and the practice continues today. Although scholars tried, they could not change, alter or

---

[11] Quran

destroy not one word or verse of this book called, "the Quran." From the time of the Prophet to today every Arabic chapter and verse of the Quran is, all the same, today as it was 1500 years ago. If you want to absolutely know what God gave and said to the last Prophet first the individual has to learn the Arabic language fluently.

Martin Luther, the leader of the Protestant Reformation, was a German monk, priest and theologian, "mister faith without work." He taught that salvation is not earned by good deeds but received only as a free gift of God's grace through faith in Jesus Christ as a redeemer from sin. This statement has some merits, in the Islamic faith the scholars state, "an individual will only get to heaven by the mercy of God," which may mean faith alone. But good deeds and works are actions of men it helps appearances and is needed although God knows the true intentions of each person. If you observe the Christian people there is no daily prayer in the Protestant churches because they are all closed. There are no good deeds beyond having polite manners or doing charitable work. The Christian faith has no rituals, no fasting, no pilgrimage to Jerusalem and most importantly, no covenant. Martin Luther is in agreement with Paul, there is no need for prayer, fasting, sacrifice, rituals and pilgrimage. On the Day of Judgment the Christians will have a big zero, or no good deeds because the foundation of Christianity rests on Paul, then Constantine, then the 15th century Monk Martin Luther. As a consequence of poor foundational understanding, new people and innovations from the many different churches are created every day. So we conclude by saying all of Christianity is in a state of blasphemy, the Catholic Church, the other orthodox churches, absolutely all of the 16th century Protestant churches and their many denominations, as well as non-trinity churches and the new non-denominational churches but worse their book, "the Bible" is in error too.

In this Christian country, we see many churches. Traditionally, churches are mostly open on Sunday for services. According to various Christian opinions, this building is responsible for representing the house of God, Jesus, the lord, and an assembly of Christian people. Today is Thursday at 1:30 pm, if an individual wanted to eat he or she can eat at home or go out in the community to a restaurant. If a person wanted to exercise he or she can exercise at home or they can go out into the community to a gym or park. If a person wanted to read a book they can read it at home or they can go out into the community to the library. If a person wanted to watch a movie, they can watch it at home or they can go out into the community to a cinema. However, if Christians wanted to pray, they can only pray at home because all of the Christian churches in the community are closed. Furthermore, to open a church the people will have to pay the piper.

It is not good to compare Islam to Christianity, but Muhammad said, "The Muslims have a religion but no men and the Christians have no religion but have men." The meaning is the Muslims have a covenant (the Kalimah, the

5 prays per day, fasting for a whole month, a poor tax and the pilgrimage to Mecca) but the men do not want to practice the task however, the Christians have no religion, no covenant, no daily pray, no fasting, no pilgrimage, no rituals nothing compulsory to practice but they have men that want to do something. If we go back to Paul, the apostle to the gentiles, he tells the gentile people you only have to believe that Jesus died for your sins and you will go to heaven and also now Martin Luther says faith without work will get you salvation. These last two statements are so weak and will have no weight, no merits on the Day of Judgment. People need religion every day like a person needs food and water. But in most Christian countries the church is only open on Sundays. The Christian people should have a place where they can escape the madness of the world and be with God alone for some time in the afternoon. Distractions like one's phone, job, car, TV, radio, stove, refrigerator, the mall, and the park are all outside of the confines of this sacred space. But this is unrealistic for today's Christian. Finally, if the present-day Christians look deep into the bible they will see that all the individual names of people are not Roman Catholics, Greek Orthodox, Anglicans, Protestants, are any of the many other sects and denominations. The New Testament should focus only on Jesus Christ's teachings, practices and how he worshipped his Lord. The New Testament should absolutely not be about Paul, or his stories, writings or opinions. Paul's strong influence results in people being followers of Paul and not the Prophet

Jesus or his twelve disciples. These followers are separated from the true reality of faith and were strategically set astray from God's path by White Christian domination.

Within the last 100 years or so, hundreds of other religions or churches started calling themselves Non-denominational. If these churches use the King James Bible, then they fall under the Protestant tradition. Some Christians have done the research and acknowledge all the white man-made Protestant denominations; therefore, non-denomination has broken off from mainstream Protestantism. The term "non-denominational" is just another division of the overarching Christian faith. These congregations follow emotional and charismatic personalities; therefore, the people can be told to believe in any concept, ideology, and philosophy that will lead to their doom. Finally, as long as the Church and Christianity continue to evolve by making new doctrines, new denominations, new alterations to scripture and implementing new dogmas and following new clever clergymen; the Christians will continue to be blinded and confused, unable to see the truth. Perfect Example Jim Jones was a charismatic man who demanded loyalty and preached sacrifice, he started an integrationist church called, "the People's Temple," with the different ethnic groups but mostly blacks in San Francisco. He became a communist, a faith-healer and then comes FBI investigation. Lastly, the church becomes an occult, Jim starts using drugs and becomes paranoid, therefore, moving the whole of the church members to Guyana. It was so sad that Black people were conditioned to follow behind white people. If you work for a white man and he signs your check then obey him. But when it comes to religion and spirituality leave the white man's concepts, theologies and ideologies along. Many congregational members brought plane tickets to fly to Guyana because the psychic Jim Jones worried about nuclear attacks from the US government especially the FBI and CIA. Furthermore, with the visit of Congressman Ryan, Jim used these factors to influence all his followers to drink cyanide-lace grape punch and died. On that day November 18, 1978, over 900 people commit "revolutionary suicide." Jim Jones died the same day possible from a self-inflicted gunshot wound.

Chapter VIII

Native Americans

Stampeding blood of hatred and violence
run from the brain to the heart to
the soul of the White Christians
but soon they will teach this
evil to the black race

The European explorers and settlers that first came to the Americas were all white Christian people. The settlers consisted of a diverse group of professionals, theologians, educated people, peasants and criminals. They all shared one commonality: the belief in the Bible or the Christian faith. If Jesus had been on one of the three ships that sailed to the New World, he would have greeted the natives with peace and converted the indigenous people to Ibrahim's monotheistic faith. Unlike the white Christians (Christopher Columbus), they would not have considered the natives to be savages and or make them slaves. Those that followed Ibrahim would not have taken the land of the natives, spread disease or ethnically cleansed the indigenous populations. Christian people affirm that they recognized and obey the Mosaic Law or the Ten Commandments, but their actions state the contrary. There is one law that says "thou shall not kill." When the white European Christians initially came to the Americas they came not with the extension of the bible but with the extension of advanced weaponry. Native

American people were not Christians, they never read the bible, and were not educated according to European standards, but they had an established culture, morals, hospitality and knowledge of how to cultivate the land. This period is the darkest of all for white European Christian people because the trajectory of history shows that their intentions were to dominate, accumulate wealth through capitalism, introduce slavery to the Americas, Christianize the natives and commit murder from the Americas to Africa, throughout India (Asia), and Australia.

Historically, it has been impossible to enslave members of societies who were nomadic hunter-gatherers, herdsmen, or fishermen. Consequently, the Europeans in North America either exterminated the warriors of the hunting tribes or forced the simple food gatherers into a labor of death. The noble "Redman" was not an effective slave because the natives of the Americas were highly susceptible to European diseases (smallpox, typhus, measles, influenza and syphilis). In search of a labor force, the evil white Christians from Europe ventured to Africa because black people were submissive and their immune systems were strong enough to resist disease.

George Washington proposed the acculturation of the Indians and Thomas Jefferson developed a policy that acknowledged the rights of Native Americans in relation to their homelands. All Indians who adopted civilized behavior by converting to Christianity were allowed to remain east of the Mississippi as long as they agreed to practice an agriculture-based society. During Andrew

Jackson's presidency, he systematically moved all surviving Native Americans to the furthest corner of the west.

British settlers had a plan. Their leaders who settled in North America were educated and their rulers were ruthless and merciless. As the peasant soldiers who did the crown's bidding invaded North America, the wealth that was accumulated across the Atlantic flowed back to Great Britain in the form of stolen goods and unjust land entitlement. The British military was very aggressive known as the "Red Coats," and the British loved to start fights, and spill blood and loved using the word "bloody" for a reason.

With so many Indian tribes, treaties, conflicts, and issues in this unreconciled history of the Native Americans, it was difficult to generalize the history. Some certainty the Native American tribes were here first, when the first settlers came they were not friendly, did not want to mix with the tribe but wanted to control and dominate. All up and down the 13 colonies there were wars and conflicts with the Natives. The settlers had a few very powerful common facts they were all white Protestant Christians, very aggressive people from Europe that carry weapons and love war, but good planning, and organization. With the support of British imperialism, the colonists were organized and able to form a stable government. However the natives were very tribal, they fought each other, living on the land, the guns are not their weapon of choice and when observed by the Europeans, the settlers detect an easy victory. Some tribes helped the settler's enemy the

British and some tribes help the settlers against other tribes in each situation the Indians were being used and manipulated.

With the Declaration of Independence issued on July 4, 1776, and after the war of 1812, most European influences and threats ended. Therefore the US government did not need to rely on and ally with any Indian tribe. The US laws and policies regarding American Indians (AI) were shaped by the often conflicting political priorities and agendas of each US President, Congress, and Supreme Court. These conflicting priorities and agendas produced conflicting and contradictory Federal Indian law problems that spread into subsequent tribal/federal/state and government jurisdictions. The US government had no true intention to bring an end to any of the many tribal conflicts and legal issues that they helped foster.

In 1776 when the founding fathers wrote the Bill of Rights and the second amendment, black slaves were in a completely submissive state and under the control of rich white capitalists. However, the Native Americans posed a threat to the white race. Manifest Destiny or the belief that white Christians were destined by God to control the Americas, led to the extermination of the Indian Nations from the 1850s to the 1870s. The Natives were seen as obstacles that needed to be reduced in order to achieve westward expansion. John O'Sullivan during the California gold rush wrote, "The individual extermination of Indians went largely unchallenged by federal government officials." There were two popular gun manufacturers during the Wild West era: Colt and Smith & Wesson. Every white man was armed and ready to murder the Natives.

The lawlessness of the 'Wild Wild West,' was encouraged by the influx of European immigrants who came to America and were told to go west. The displaced Indians were no longer on the Atlantic coast, they found new homes for their endangered tribes inland spanning from North Dakota to Texas and the Great Plains. They continued to hunt and follow the Buffalo (Bison), lived in tepees, rode horses, engaged in agriculture, and grew tobacco. Once again, the civility of the natives would be challenged by the white Christians who ventured across the Great Plains in wagons with greed on their minds. The government provided land grants and subsidies to the new frontiersmen to establish farms and ranches to "improve the land." In the local town many (black and white) men were fur traders, miners, cowboys, scouts, woodsmen, farmhands, saloon workers, cooks, and outlaws and the women in town worked as prostitutes. Church services on Sunday were for whites only.

The frontier was full of crime and extreme violence, dueling, crimes of drunkenness, selling whiskey to the Indians, horse stealing, counterfeiting, highway robbery of stagecoaches, and the three on one or a solitary man on his horse being robbed, horseless and worse murdered. Next, there were two types of bandits the Mexican and Indians who target white opportunity along the Mexico border, particularly in Texas, Arizona and California. The second group and maybe the worse of the two, the American famous outlaws of the west including Jesse James, Billy the Kid, the Dalton Gang, Butch Cassidy and the Wild Bunch and hundreds of others who preyed on banks, trains and stagecoaches. These men were madmen, ex-confederate soldiers, misfits, drifters, and gunslingers; they hate the new Yankee government. After entering a town to commit a crime the people raised a posse to attempt to drive them out or capture them. Although these cowboys probably never read the bible or entered a church, in their death they were considered Christian because the preacher most likely said the trinity over their bodies. At the close of this century, treaties were made and broken, American Indian reservations were encroached upon and by 1900, the depopulation of the American Indians decreased by 90%.

Below charts are some of the well-known Indian tribes, the year of the ending conflicts, the opponent, the place and end results, reservation also means treaties and the US government recognized them and had direct contact with.

Tribe	Year	Opponent	Place	Results
Powhatan	1622	Settlers	Maryland Virginia	diseases Massacre
Mohican	1830	Settlers	Albany, NY	Massacre
Seneca	1797	USA	Western,NY	Reservation
Mohawk	1794	USA	NY &Canada	Reservation
Susquehannock	1763	Settlers	East Coast	Massacre

Iroquois	1830	USA	Northeast	Relocation
Kiowa	1858, Texas Rangers		Oklahoma,Tx	Relocation
Apache	1862	US army	New Mexico	Reservation
Comanche	1867	US govt.	GreatPlains	Reservation
Sioux	1876	US army	Montana,Wy	Reservation
Navajo	1864	US army	NewMexico	Reservation
Cheyenne and killed	1879	US army	GreatPlains	Recaptured
Lakota	1851	US army	GreatPlains	Reservation
Cherokee	1830	US armySoutheasternstates		Oklahoma
Chickasaw	1830	US armySoutheasternstates		Reservation
Choctaw	1830	US armySoutheasternstates		Reservation
Muscogee Creek	1830	US armySoutheasternstates		Reservation
Seminole	1830	US armySoutheasternstates		Reservation
Incas disease	1618	Spanish	Peru,Chile,Bolivia	Slaughter
Aztecs Empire	1519	Spanish	Central Mexico	Massacred disease
West Indies tribes	1542	Spanish	Caribbean	Slaughter

Andrew Jackson, the man on the $20 bill, defeated the Creek Indians in 1814 at the Battle of Horseshoe Bend and the British at the Battle of New Orleans. These battles consisted of the continuation of the ethnic cleansing of

Native Americans and the forced relocation of tribes from the southeast to the west of the Mississippi River. Jackson was a wealthy slaveholder who supported slavery and the removal of Indians. The 1830 Indian Removal Act caused five tribal nations to move west of the Mississippi River to another US territory. The continual cession from white squatters preceded the threat of military force called the "Trail of Tears." Various tribes suffered from harsh weather, diseases and starvation while making the arduous trek to land far away from their place of origin.

The Battle of the Little Bighorn on June 25-26, 1876 was the first battle that included Native American tribes (Lakota, Cheyenne, Arapahoe) working together to successfully defeat General George Custer's and his 7th Cavalry regiment of the United States Army. Credit must be given to Sitting Bull, Crazy Horse, Chief Gall, and Lame White Man for annihilating five of the seven companies. Earlier in the same month, on June 17, 1876, the Sioux, Lakota and Cheyenne were victorious in their alignment in the Battle of the Rosebud.

The Wounded Knee massacre in South Dakota occurred on December 29, 1890, on a three-day freezing cold blizzard snowy afternoon and consider the last of the American Indian Wars. In one version because Black Coyote was reluctant to give up his rifle during the disarmament of the Lakota people a scuffle started a shot was fired which resulted in the 7th cavalry's opening fire indiscriminately from all sides killing men, women, and children as well as some of their own fellow troopers using four Hotchkiss guns. Victory for the 7th US cavalry murdering over 90 men, 200 unarmed women and children, and 51 wounded in close range. Some surviving women and babies attached to their mother were found by the burial party three days later frozen dead. The results of the proud white Protestant Christian government and their American public were also in favor, with one white man saying, "The pioneer's safety depends upon the total extermination of the Indians." In a telegram after the war, General Miles said, "The difficult Indian problem cannot be solved permanently at this end of the line. It requires the fulfillment of Congress of the treaty obligations that the Indians were entreated and coerced into signing. They signed away a valuable portion of their reservation and it is now occupied by white people for which they had received nothing."[12]

The Native Americans were God's creatures too, they have every right to exist, practice their culture and be themselves. The white Protestant Christians first defeated, the British, with help from the slaves, then diseased and massacred the Atlantic coast Indians with help from the Buffalo soldiers. The Buffalo Soldiers first were a Black men regiment only to serve west of the Mississippi River because of the prevailing attitudes of the white confederates following the Civil War. Their objectives were to protect the white settlers as they moved west, and to support the westward expansion by building the infrastructure needed for new settlements to flourish.

---

[12] Internet: Wikipedia.org

Here the Buffalo soldiers protecting the race of people that truly hated them and had to enslave them just 25 years ago. Not one Buffalo soldier receive one acre of land after the depopulation and cleansing of the Indians from the plains. However, the Indians were friendly and hospitable to the Black man, but the Indians did not understand why the black man behaved the same as the white man in their attempts to carry out the genocide of the Natives. The Indians did not understand that the Black was enslaved, whipped/beaten, acculturated/assimilated, and Christianized by white Europeans. All of this ill-treatment equated to a 100% submissive creature known as the Black man. He may appear to be Black, but his soul has been indoctrinated with white values of hatred, violence, cruelty and bigotry.

The US government played dangerous games with the uneducated Natives. Evidence of this was the implementation of many treaties that robbed natives of their land, allowing US territories to be established. White European Christians truly believed that the land from New York City to California was theirs and the rights granted to them by the US Constitution allowed them to murder, kill, and massacre Indians. Also, it is written that white Protestant Christians said, they have a God-given right to the land, do they have a God-given right to murder too? The confession of guilt or sin of white Protestant dominance is supported by the Founding Fathers' Bill of Rights, white Presidents, white elected officials and the protection from the US cavalry, but it is clear that they did not have God's blessing. At the time of their deaths and on the Day of Judgment, these white people will enter through a door that will have the word "Hell" on it.

The name "reservation" comes from the conception of the Indian tribes as independent sovereigns at the time the U.S. Constitution was ratified. Thus, the early peace treaties (often signed under) in which Indian tribes surrendered large portions of land to the U.S. also designated parcels which the tribes, as sovereigns, "reserved" to themselves, and those parcels came to be called "reservations." The term remained in use even after the federal government began to forcibly relocate tribes to parcels of land to which they had no historical connection. What was the underlying significance of the reservations? One, to absolutely control, dominate, and take their freedom and humiliate them, too, Frank Baum wrote, "Having wronged them for centuries, we had better, in order to protect our civilization, follow it up by one more wrong and wipe these untamed and untamable creatures from the face of the earth."[13]

After the many Indian wars, genocide, land seizures, imprisonment on reservations, obliteration of the various native languages with English, and the wrongful conversion to Christianity, Native Americans and white Christian people will never be brothers, but always enemies. These European Americans, who profess faith in Christianity, were not true believers or followers of Jesus Christ. It is not good to compare the white Christian with

---

[13] Editor Frank Baum

the Arab Muslims of North Africa and with the Berber people. The Arab Muslims did completely dominate and converted the Berbers to Islam but the difference, history does not say the Arab Muslims slaughter them or massacred or make them indigenous. In fact the Arab Muslims inter-married with the Berbers, prayed together, military pursuits; the children went to school together, no treaties, no separation, and no reservations. They both lived in peace, and harmony and practiced integration and tolerance. To complicate matters, the U.S. government, a white Christian racist organization, loves to dominate the people they hate and disparage vulnerable peoples for life. The U.S. government forced the Native Americans into signing and obeying the many treaties. And it was the U.S. government that allowed individual states to violate treaties without consequence. According to martial law, as the members of individual Native American nations, they were not automatically citizens and had no standing in any U.S. court.

Finally to be disgraced first, to be conquered, secondly, the wars ended in slaughtered and massacred, thirdly the change in livelihood, catching an incurable white man disease, the loss of your tribal territory, learning new vain behaviors and fourthly the worse to become Christian, drinking white man's alcohol but one more disgraceful factor when your enemy the white Christians makes movies about the Native and or indigenous people.

Know that the white people were authors of

history. They make themselves the villains at the beginning of the movie and heroes or protagonists at the end and the Natives are victimized in the beginning and the antagonist or the bad guy at the end. Mostly all western movies portrayed Native American or Indians as uncivilized and savage villains. This crystallized the image of "Indians" as dangerous and unacceptable to live amongst. They show the Native wearing clothes made from animal skins, carrying spears, and knives and having to fight with all strangers who came to their land. These movies also created strong stereotypes which encouraged racism. And one more humongous disgracing was the making them the mascots of many sports teams which was very disrespectful and offensive.

Examples:

NFL:	**Mascots**
Washington	"Redskins"
Kansas City	"Chiefs"
Baseball:	
Atlantic	"Braves"
Cleveland	"Indians"
Basketball:	
Golden State	"Warriors"
Canadian Football:	
Edmonton	"Eskimos"
Junior Ice Hockey:	
Chicago	"Blackhawks"
Portland	"Winterhawks"

Also, thousands of more Indian mascots in other

sports and on the College level and the High School levels were in usage. The National Congress of American Indians issued a resolution opposing the continued usage of native team names, mascots and logos. In 2002 a poll done by Sports Illustrate resulted in 83% of American Indians saying, that professional teams should not stop using Indian nicknames, mascots or symbols. Finally, The Indians can beat the drum in lamentation regarding the loss of land and culture, the political issues that they have faced, and the humiliation that they have seen in Hollywood and in organized sports. But they have no representative in Washington and as long as the white Christians continue to dominate the Native Americans, they will always be considered the Redman, an indigenous relic, and as white Christians like to say, at the bottom of the "totem pole."

The Native Americans should organize a committee where all the tribes and Nations unite with their treaty agreements, issues of government promises and other documents. They should have a signed petition and a large number of supporters to aid in the presentation of their issues. Complaints should be brought to Capitol Hill and Congress and the Senate should be forced to provide a resolution, monetary retribution, and an end to all of the complications that the Natives have endured. If the government does not comply, then all the Indian nations should show solidarity and march on Washington, followed by a declaration of war.

Chapter IX

The Most Unholy, Unmerciful and Cruelest Bloody Creatures on the Face of the Earth the British Empire

The definition of a Christian is any white person born in Europe (England, France Spain, Italy, Germany, and Portugal). During the slavery, colonization and inquisitional periods, if a person never entered a church, but fought in the Christian wars, sailed on Christian fleets and died in the name of the trinity, the individual was still considered a Christian. In general, all the European countries practiced and benefited from slavery, aggressive domination and the usurpation of territories in Africa, South East Asia, and the Americas. From 1600 to 1800, the capitalistic English monarchy experienced rampant crime. England endured hundreds of rapes, murders, public drunkenness, aiding, abetting, assault, battery, theft and larceny. Citizens armed themselves with deadly weapons as the English population continued to grow with wickedness and polytheism. As a remedy, it was decided that criminals would be transported to the many new colonies. The expelled prisoners brought perversion with them into the new colonies. Because misery loves company, the whites persuaded and encouraged the natives to accept and practice the evil social vices of the white Christians and white behaviors.

Historically, the British Empire is the most destructive of peoples, cultures, customs, heritage, livelihoods and lands. They are the atrocious epitome of imperialism. The British Empire comprised the colonies, the dominions, protectorates, mandates, and other territories all ruled and administered by the United Kingdom. History says from the British perspective that it was the largest empire in the world, a global power, dominated countries on four continents, controlled one-fifth of the world's population, a quarter of the earth's total landmass and at the peak of its dominance, it was often said that, "the sun never sets on the British Empire." However, if reading the history from the British point of view, (all their aggressive invasions, the wars, their superior weaponry causing slaughter, massacre of native people and worse the filthy sailors, the diseases they carry on their bodies and shared with the natives that cause health epidemics and the killing of thousands of native people), they did nothing wrong. But from the natives in the Americas to Africa, to India and South East Asia not one region asks or welcomes the invasion of the British Empire. The invasions can be seen as the wrath of God, a curse, and destructive punishment of all the people the British made connection with.

England is a very small country, with a large population of Protestants who were once rooted in Catholicism. When sailing to the Caribbean, their first objective was to establish a colony and or a trading post. It was taken for granted that if the island was populated, guns and cannons would be used to depopulate the natives. When sailing to large countries like Australia, New

Zealand, South Africa, Canada and the USA, if inhabitants were not initially seen, the Brits would give the land a name; claim it as a British colony, dominated by British sovereignty and the monarch. Now the curse, because the British see the native people who are non-white, non-Christian, and have their own culture/customs and because the British had government power, military power, diseased power, they made laws that benefit their lifestyle that went against the Natives. The British Empire's behavior around the world interacting with other countries was like a three-year-old having a tantrum, if treaties did not satisfy British interest or their goals of improved trade and diplomatic relations, the outcome, the British would seize outright and use military power to violently enforce their will or redress.

The British used four successful attributes in conquering, dominating and changing the native people: weapons of mass destruction, their sovereignty in the creation of laws, imperialism and Christianity. Once the older generation was depleted, extinct or submissive, the education of the new colonized generation took place. Customs and traditions that were established prior to British dominance were cast aside and the new generation learned about the English way of life and the concept of Christianity that leads to the destruction of souls.

The British Empire in their world voyage extremely despised the Muslims and the Islamic world. One, the Muslims of Africa and Southeast Asia world understood aggression, two, they know the history of the Christian first Crusaders attacking and slaughtering the Muslim citizens, three, the people are educated, and they have a government, military and strong faith. However, the core of British intelligence has always been to rule through orchestrated conflicts and wars and also to blame its crimes on others in the media and worse the ignorant people see the British as the good guys. The peaceful people of the world were not prepared for his hateful, violent aggressive bloody white madman.

It is said, that Queen Victoria of the British Empire, only took baths three times a year. If the Queen only took a bath three times a year, how many baths did the regular population take? It is a fact that all of the sails on the fleets traveling the world carried deadly viruses and infections. Sailors and convicts contaminated healthy people with smallpox, syphilis, measles and influenza. Before the arrival of the dominating white European Christians, the Aboriginals lived along the shoreline. Here they practiced fishing, hunting, and harvesting around the bush, and they were very self-sufficient. They worked harmoniously with the land, free of disease and rich with a complex ritual lifestyle of language, customs, spirituality and trade with other tribes. With the colonization of Australia beginning in 1788, a series of European epidemic diseases such as measles, smallpox, and tuberculosis claimed the lives of an estimated 90% of the Darug people by 1789. The arrogant and ignorant Lt. James Cook, the first explorer to the island, declared the land "New South Wales" and the property of Britain's King George ignoring the 400 or more aborigine nations living there.

Since the invasion in 1788, the conquered Aborigine people were oppressed by a world unnatural to their existence for thousands of years. Pacification by force culminated in the late 1880s, leading to a massive depopulation and extinction for some groups. By the 1940s almost all aborigines were Christianized and assimilated into rural and urban Australian society as low-paid laborers with limited rights. Many aborigine children were taken from their natural parents and given to white foster parents to promote assimilation. Just two years after the conquest of these peaceful people, the complete taking of the Australia Island, next is the depopulation and the many massacres.

In 1790 Governor Arthur Phillip issued an order for a party of non-commissioned officers to bring in six natives near Botany Bay or put the number to death. In 1803 the first British colonist arrived (prisoners, soldiers, volunteers and diseases) the prisoners escaped. On the loose, they randomly killed the natives and raped their women, with sadistic killing chopping off the heads and forcing the wife to carry it on around her neck. In 1816 the Aborigines the Gundungurra and Dharawal could not sustain themselves because of the white farms moving in and taking all the land. British soldiers were ordered by Governor Macquaries to use their horses to force men, women and children to fall from the cliffs of the gorge to their deaths below. The cape grim massacre in 1828 when four shepherds with muskets ambushed 30 unarmed

Tasmanian, the aborigine men were shot on sight and the women were seized to serve the needs of the shepherds and sealers many of whom took two aboriginal women each. White Christian people are not your brothers and sisters in Christ and they are not your friends when it comes to business ventures if a non-white comes close to a white female surely he will lose his life.

In 1829 the Governor used their prisoners to hunt down the natives and a $5.00 reward was offered for every native that was retrieved. The Black War is recorded as a genocide resulting in the elimination of the full-blooded Tasmanian Aborigine population in 1830. A chain of 5000 white soldiers set out to corner all the natives into a small space, for several weeks the chain moved across the whole island and in the end, just 300 natives remained.

The indigenous people of the world tried to maintain their rights as people despite deprivation, assimilation, and genocide. Each indigenous culture is distinct and unique. While many people may express similar worldviews and common indigenous identities, their cultures are nonetheless based on different histories, environments, and creative spirits. Indigenous peoples live in every region of the world. They live in climates ranging from Arctic cold to Sahara hot and often claim a deep connection to their lands and natural environments. For many indigenous peoples, the natural world is a valued source of food, health, spirituality and identity. The land is both a critical resource that sustains life and a major cause of struggle and even death.

The aborigine people of East Gippsland, Victoria, Australia, known as the Gunai/Kurnai people, fought against the European invasion of their land. The technical superiority of the Europeans' weapons gave the Europeans an absolute advantage. At least 300 people were killed, but other figures estimate up to 1,000. However, it is extremely difficult to be certain about the real death toll as so few records still exist or were even made at the time. Diseases introduced in the 1820s by European sealers and whalers also caused a rapid decline in Aborigine numbers. The following list was compiled from such things as letters and diaries.

Domination through genocide and white Christian aggressive superiority over these Black people in 1833-34 is seen in the convincing ground massacre recorded as the largest massacre in Victoria by the Whalers who used the musket gun to kill over 200 women and children. In 1834 the Battle of Pinjarra, over 25 aborigines were murdered. In 1836 a proud LT. Bunbury shot 11 Aborigine men and the settlers in the district collected ears of the Aborigine men who were slain. In 1838 the Waterloo Creek Massacre was ordered by Sydney's policemen who attacked an encampment of Kamilaroi people in the remote bushland. Bunbury's men murdered over three hundred natives, therefore wiping out the tribe. In 1839 the assistant protector of the Aborigine region wrote, that the massacre by the settlers and Charles Hutton was "a deliberately planned illegal reprisal." Each year massacres were led by white Christian settlers and supported by their white Christian government officials and the monarch in England. Furthermore, the settlers used poison to kill 50 aborigines in the Brisbane Valley.

Year	Name of massacre	kills	Tribe or place
1842	Evans Head Massacre	100	Bundjalung tribe's people
1843	Warrigal Creek	100-150	aborigines
1846	George Smythe's surveying party shot 7 to 9 Aborigines in cold blood		
1850	massacre of the Yeeman	300	killed by the police and the public
1861	In Queensland	170	aborigines
1865	in Western Australia	20	aborigines
1867	Gouilbolba Hill massacre	300	men, women and children
1868	Flying Foam Massacre	20-150	Yaburara aborigines
1874	Borrow Creek Massacre	90	Northern Territory
1875	Blackfellow's Creek Massacre, Far North Queensland		
1879	Cape Bedford	28	Guugu-Yimidhirr tribe
1880	Arnhem Land, Yolngu people were fed poisoned horse meat.		

1884   Battle Mountain   200 Kalkadoon people murder

1887, 1890 Hall Creek, Spreewah Massacre unconfirmed atrocities occurred

1900's The Killing Times, from 1890 to 1920

1906-7 Canning stock route Aborigines were raped, massacred, tortured,

1915   Mistake Creek Massacre all over a cow that was found after the massacre   7 Kija people killed

1918   Bentinck Island the Kaiadit men were shot, women raped, and drowned

1924   Bedford Downs Massacre

1926   Forrest River Massacre

1928   Coniston Massacre   32 Northern territory by white dingo trapper

Also by the hands of the Bloody British, in 1899-1902 in South Africa, 28,000 Afrikaner women and children died in British concentration camps.

INDIA: British Indian Holocaust

1.8 billion excess deaths, 1757-1947; 10 million killed in post-1857 Indian Mutiny reprisals; 1 million starved, 1895-1897 Indian Famine; 6-9 million starved, 1899-1900 Indian Famine.

IRAQ: British Suppression of the Arab Revolt in Iraq

British invaded in 1914. The bombing of Kurds using poison gas in the 1920s

INDONESIA: A Million Deaths

Bloodbath in Indonesia begins as the army moves against supporters of the Indonesian Communist Party, reaching around a million deaths. Declassified documents show Britain aids the Indonesian army in conducting the slaughter through covert operations and secret messages of support.

AFRICA: Gukurahundi Massacres (Zimbabwe)

Britain was behind the 1980s massacres that left nearly 30,000 innocent civilians from Matabeleland and the Midlands dead.

newbritishempire.site11.com/british-massacres.html

The information on this list is all the facts written by the white Australians. In this period of Aboriginal history, not one white settler was ever accused, charged or arrested for murdering and killing these native people all a crime against humanity. The ultimate disgrace of the aboriginal people came in 1931 from the many raped women; the white racist government started stealing the mixed-race aboriginal children from their mothers taking them more than 1500 miles from their native settlement. The objective was to 100% acculturate/assimilate and Christianize these children into mainstream society. Sadly today the unsubstantially aboriginal people are conditional second to third-class citizens in their country of Australia. They have lost all of their customs and culture because of war, acculturation, assimilation and Christianization. They understand English, being an Individualist, a capitalist;

they know how to steal, lie, cheat, drink alcohol, use drugs, beat one's spouse and worse like the British criminals that colonize the island today that are the criminals that populate the jails and prisons.

There is very little evidence to back up any of these claims. Gippsland, Henry Meyrick wrote in a letter home to his relatives in England in 1846: [14]

> *The blacks are very quiet here now, poor wretches. No wild beast of the forest was ever hunted down with such unsparing perseverance as they are. Men, women and children are shot whenever they can be met with ... I have protested against it at every station I have been in Gippsland, in the strongest language, but these things are kept very secret as the penalty would certainly be hanging ... For myself, if I caught a black actually killing my sheep, I would shoot him with as little remorse as I would a wild dog, but no consideration on earth would induce me to ride into a camp and fire on them indiscriminately, as is the custom whenever the smoke is seen. They [the Aborigines] will very shortly be extinct. It is impossible to say how many have been shot, but I am convinced that not less than 450 have been murdered altogether.*

What kind of human beings were these white Christian British that they can murder at will with no conscious, liability and mercy? In a world where white

---

[14] Internet: Wikipedia.org

Christians continue to rule, dominate; dictate have all the military capability to continue to destroy lives and blame the innocent and the weak. The people must believe in the unseen God correctly but not any of the trinity gods of Christianity. These people will not and will never get international justice from any of the white Christian organizations just as the United Nations, the British Parliament, The Hague, and or Geneva. God has created man to be higher in spirituality than the angels however, man has fallen lower than the animals, example the British people are all on the level of the "Tasmanian Devil," with their extremely loud screech sound, a pure carnivorous, that maims then ferocity eats its prey.

Justice will only come on the Day of Judgment through God's eyes and hands. Pray that the God of Ibrahim will accept the Aborigines, the many indigenous, Native Americans and others that were considered non-Muslims in His Heaven and punish the British Christians, European Christians and other Christians that aggressively murder-kill-slaughter and massacre unarmed people all over the world, for surely they broke the six commandments, "thou shalt not kill."

In India, early Muslim conquests made limited inroads in the Rajput Kingdom of the 7th century, but the major Muslim conquest took place from the 13th to the 16th centuries. The Mughal Empire ruled the Indian subcontinent from 1526 to 1757, these ethnic people are descendants of Genghis Khan's grandson Timur. During this period India enjoyed much cultural, and economic progress as well as religious harmony. The Rajput Kingdom had posed a significant threat to the Mughal dominance but they were all subdued. Although the Muslim minority-dominated, and the Islamic faith was extremely opposite to the Hindu faith the people had an understanding of each other and live in peace but by the mid-18th century. The Mughal Empire became weak from Muslims fighting within, threats from Marathas, Rajputs, Sikhs and Jats mostly Hindu people and being defeated in 1739 by the Persian Shia Muslims, Nader Shah in the Battle of Karnal. However, the British trading company (the British East India Company) was presently trading in India but they do not rule but after the battle of Plassey in 1757 they rule Bengal.

The Muslims and the Hindus did not like the dominating presence of the British. The people of India had disdain for the arrogance, greed and abuses of the British. The mutiny of infantry that consisted of mostly Hindu soldiers within the East India Company's army resulted in the Indian Rebellion of 1857. The sword remained the weapon of choice for the Muslims and Hindus, but the British used rifles. Although to make the battle somewhat fair, the Muslims and Hindus were given rifles. This was a problem because the soldier had to bite off the paper cartridges made from pig grease and fat that contained the gunpowder. This action that was needed for adequate self-defense was rejected due to the religious beliefs of Muslims and Hindus; the results were thousands of casualties and losses on the side of the Muslims and

Hindus. Furthermore, both faiths did not have the military strategy, tactics and skills needed to fight with guns. This is the curse this is the omen, from the small east (British) company ruling to the British crown ruling.

The British Empire disapproved of the minority Muslim rule. But in Britain's first 100 years of ruling, they make up less than one percent of the population. Unlike the Australian Aborigine, or the Native Americans and or the South Africans the Indians were more than willing to serve and work for the British. And the British took complete advantage of this cheap and ignorant labor. The conquest of India was like finding a field of apple trees but instead, the tree had gold bars ready for the picking. India was a far greater industrial and manufacturing nation than any in Europe, Africa or any country in Asia. India was coveted for textile goods: the fine products of heirloom, cotton, wools, linen and silk were famous all over the civilized world. Exquisite Indian jewelry and precious stones cut in every lovely form, pottery, porcelain, ceramic of every kind, quality, color and beautiful shape; metal, iron, steel, silver and gold nurtured the greed of the British Empire. India's grand architecture was superior in beauty to any in the world. The engineers, merchants, great businessmen, bankers and financiers readily adopted capitalism. Not only was India the greatest ship-building nation, but commerce and trade by land and sea were extended to all known civilized countries. Such was the India which the British found and furthermore, the drain of India's wealth to England in the sum of over five billion dollars. This stolen wealth supplied England with free capital for the development of mechanical inventions and made the industrial revolution possible.

The prosperity of the British bureaucracy, aristocracy (the Brahman) citizens at the top, and Sudras are the Dalits (also called Untouchables) the pauper and emasculated Indians at the bottom a picture of poverty and ugliness of British rule. The British treated the Hindus as strangers and foreigners in India, in a manner quite as unsympathetic, harsh and abusive.

Because of business decisions and the way the British farm, the British colonial masters used to hunger and starvation as tools to depopulate the Muslims in Bengal for about eighteen decades which claimed about 30 million lives. In 1919 the Jallianwala Bagh massacre, the British police open fire on Sikhs and Hindus protesting killing approximately 1000 people. The Malabar rebellion/riots in Southern India (1921) included the belligerent Hindus and the British Raj against Mappila's Muslims. The issues of unfair land ownership, privileges, rights and obligations solely for the British led to an upheaval where 100,000 casualties were lost on both sides, 50,000 Muslims were imprisoned and 10,000 were counted as missing. In 1930 the Qissa Khwani bazaar massacre by British police killed 400-700 Hindus and Muslims in Peshawar. Lastly the Indian Holocaust, the complete perpetrator of the British Bloody Empire 1.8 billion deaths between 1757 thru 1947, 10 million killed in post-1857 Indian Mutiny reprisals, the many famines from

1895 to 1900 well over 25 million starving men, women, pregnant women, children, babies, fetus all by the hand and brains of the most unmerciful and cruel bloody creature on earth the British Empire.

The Portuguese Inquisition in Goa, India 1560 to 1774, not the country of Portugal in Europe but in India a Hindu country. First, after the Portuguese conquered and colonizing of Goa, second, forced conversions of Hindus and Muslims to Roman Catholicism, and now the inquisition forced the individuals to practice Catholicism and punished all apostate New Christians mostly Muslims, Hindus and Jews who were now suspected of practicing their original faiths in secret. Some 16,202 people were brought to trial by the inquisition some people were sentenced to death, executed, massacred, or burned in effigy, some lesser punishment or penance but the fate of most is unknown. Most of the Goa inquisitions records were destroyed by the Catholic Church after its abolition in 1812, the disgrace of the Catholic Church, so much spilled blood, massacres, unfairness, and injustice, just a humongous blot on the history of the Roman Catholic Church.

The British Empire treated the colonized Muslim countries a little differently, after defeating them in battle and destroying the military, next was the politics and the rulers but most important the British went deep into the socialization, economics and status of the people. Islam has an egalitarian system for the believers (Muslims) men. The traditions of Islam are overwhelmingly against privilege by descent, birth, status, wealth or even by race. Islam insists that rank and honor are determined only by piety and merit. Islam did recognize certain social inequalities which were master/slave, man/woman and believer/unbeliever. However, the Quran gives rights to the slave, the women and unbelievers. The Quran encourages the freeing of slaves and how to ethically treat a slave. The Quran says, "Men are only physically stronger than women and they can own property." God wants the unbelievers to become Muslims and go to heaven. But in the eyes of the British, women, slaves and unbelievers were all inferior subjects, vulnerable to strict enforcements, social disabilities and limitations that affect daily life. Therefore, the British and European powers demanded the abolition of the position of legal inferiority assigned to Christians and incidentally also to Jews in the Islamic states. All means at the disposal of Europeans were used to persuade Muslim governments to grant equality to all the subjects.

To forbid what God permits is almost as great an offense as to permit what God forbids. Slavery was a big part of the economy of the Muslim world and was authorized and regulated by the Sharia therefore a difficult task to the end. First, the British focused on the emancipation of the white Christian slaves and their origins from Greek, Georgian and Caucasian lands. Next to prohibit the trafficking of black slaves leaving Africa and moving to the Arab Empire, finally communicate and put pressure on the powers (the Ottoman Empire, Persians and North Africans) governments to reach a compromising agreement.

According to the Quran and the Sharia, there were many laws for the non-Muslim citizens of an Islamic state, the 'Dhimma' allows rights to Christians and Jews in return for taxes. The non-Muslims were excused or excluded from specific duties assigned to Muslims and otherwise equal under the laws of property, contract and obligation. An example the Sharia laws permit the consumption of pork and alcohol by Christians and Jews. In 1798 Napoleon Bonaparte's expedition and administration in Egypt drew extensively on the service of Coptic Christians, he could not tolerate the continuance of the numerous restrictions and disabilities imposed by Muslim laws on Christian subjects therefore, the 'Dhimma' were abolished. Although the French's presence in Egypt was short the Christians obtained a position considerably better than equal. Now the weak Ottoman government under pressure from the western powers indicates abolishing two more major laws, the Jizya or poll taxes and the ban on bearing arms. The Arab world did not like these new reform charters, the Imperial Rescript of 1856, which outline the full equality of all Ottomans irrespective of religion.

White Christian's aggressive domination when will it end? In the mid-nineteenth century, the white European Christian powers forced the Muslim countries to give their Christian inhabitants equality in society. During this same time period in England a white Roman Catholic and or

Protestant country there were zero Muslims living there, the same for France a white Roman Catholic country having zero Muslims living there, the same for Germany zero Muslims there and all of western Europe countries had zero Muslim population. However in the early 15th century after the many wars in Spain, Muslims did live in Spain and also ruled but white Christian domination kicked in, wars, forced Christianization and then the inquisition and ultimately completely forced removal of non-whites and non-Christians from the continent of Europe. White Christian people honor the country (King/Queen) first. The concept of believing in God, and obeying God is further down the list. Surely, the white Christian people do not fear God and have no understanding of the Day of Judgment. Also during this same period, there were no Hindus or Buddhists in Europe and no Jews in Spain, France and England.

Chapter X

Jim Crow

During this period white Christian people
attended the church regularly
Jesus preaches no hatred, no violence
so what Bible these people reading from
On the street the white race inflicts
hatred, hostility, bigotry
Complete domination over non-white people
and this is all learned ethics that starts
at the government level

Because of the person's name, in college, it took me a long time to grasp the concept, of "Jim Crow." However, after college, I overheard a man describing Jim Crow, "The image of Jim crow was a recent ex-slaved man that wore a purple jacket, green shirt, brown tie, yellow pants, potato holes in his socks and possible no shoes." They had administrative jobs given to them from the Union North to frustrate the southern whites in which it did. Then I was confused again. A carpetbagger (derogatory term) was a Yankee (Northern) carrying luggage made of carpet traveling in the south during the reconstruction era. He was a pure opportunist, exploiter and republican manipulator preying on the mostly illiterate Negro population's financial and power gains. These crafty and insidious carpetbaggers meddle in local politics, they brought land at extremely low prices and before reconstruction ended all of the Southern states and their people were taken advantage of.

The systematic enslavement of Blacks in America continues to affect the Black community even in this day and age. The methods and tools used to mentally and physically control slaves go far beyond bondage. Social structures within the black community were designed by whites where obscene, schisms were made according to gradations of skin color, pitting the old against the young, the emasculation of men, the sexual exploitation of women, the maintenance of an illiterate and uneducated black population and miscegenation. White persuasion and influence made slaves dependent on the white race and all blacks had to live in a state of subservience. The Black man's spirit and psychic were broken in many ways, one being the breaking of the horse method. This method involves the vicious whipping of the black in front of a group of particular women that he slept with. The result of this humiliation is that the women will produce a submissive child who will be more susceptible to the control and domination of their white master. This scientific process of man-breaking (horse-breaking) and instilling hate in blacks in regard to their peers was made popular by a British man by the name of "Willie Lynch" of Virginia in 1712. The Black Sambo creature is an example of a completely submissive black man that loves the white race more than he loves his mother. These types of men were created during slavery and this submissive attitude survived during Jim Crow and still exists.

Although Africans had slaves and Arabs had slaves

but history does not say they used such methods to absolutely control the mind, body and soul of a human being. But only in America by white dominating Christian people. The black race continues to suffer from this horrific era and today this method is used with different psychological methods that are supported by secular influences and Christianity. And furthermore, this psychological method is being used all over the world today to destroy civilization and create conflicts within ethnicity.

In 1859, three colorful ethnic groups were the cause of major culture clashes in America. The dominating Christians from Europe were the ruling force. Imperialism pervaded the country's government and military. The enslaved black people from Africa had no power and they were the labor force that allowed America to be a successful imperialistic power. Finally, the Native Americans struggled to survive and maintain what was left of their culture on reservations. Surviving the middle passage, the whippings, the chains, starvation, disease, the weather and lying in human waste, furthermore, centuries of terror, humiliation, vilification and deprivation. After slavery and during the Jim Crow period, the Negro people assimilated into a segregated and racially intolerant society by gaining education, inventing innovative technologies, farming, laboring and pursuing entrepreneurship. The problems were intricated from the over 150 years of slavery, 100 years of Jim Crow, intimidation, humiliation, then the acculturation/assimilation and worse Christianization. The Civil War led the freed slaves into the Reconstruction Era where many Negros excelled, but the economic freedom that was available to Blacks as citizens were thwarted by angry white southerners.

During the Civil War, on January 1, 1863, the Emancipation Proclamation was issued by President Abraham Lincoln as an executive. The proclamation ended slavery in the Confederate South and proclaimed that all slaves were forever free. On April 14, 1865, just after the Confederacy surrendered, President Abraham Lincoln was shot by a fanatical southerner, John W. Booth, at Ford's Theatre in Washington, DC. He died the following day. The Reconstruction Era for the nation included Lincoln's plan of unifying the north and south states and helping both blacks and whites adjust to an integrated society. With the end of the Civil War and the passing of the Thirteenth Amendment, slavery was made illegal in December of 1865.

The freedman's Bureau act provisions for land, the civil rights act of 1866, giving black citizens civil rights equal to those of whites, the reconstruction act, voting rights, 1868 the fourteenth amendment, definite citizenship and protecting civil rights from state interference and by 1869 twenty Negro's were serving in the house of representative and next the Fifteenth Amendment, the right to vote. The US Congress those people in Washington were passing some excellent and well-needed laws for these Negro folks. However, the

Republican Party and the next president Andrew Johnson vetoed some of the acts. But during the Reconstruction Period, the Negro will learn that they are dealing with white racist cruel evil educated and organized Christians. Escaping from white domination was impossible because white people were the Presidents, the Governors, the Mayors and the legislative branch, executive branch, and judicial branch. States were empowered to pass, enforce and interpret the laws and they did violate the Constitution. And these people were not just, fair, righteous, or morally correct. The Negro people slightly gained social mobility as seen with the trailblazing 20 black representatives in Congress. However, many Union troops in the south had to protect the Negro people from the intimidation and physical violence imparted by whites. In 1901, the last black representative lost his seat in Congress. It would be 30 years before a black person could gain a seat in the House or Senate.

After ten years of reconstruction, the implementation of Jim Crow laws and the start of the white Christian terrorist organization in the Ku Klux Klan, the white former slave owners had effectively nullified the civil right act of 1866. The Jim Crow notion of "separate but equal" facilities for whites and blacks was supported by the Supreme Court, the highest court in the land with the ruling case of "Plessey v. Ferguson". The result confirmed the immoral bias that was written in the Constitution by the principal white Christians of America, the founding fathers. This is pure white Christian domination.

From the 1880s into the 1960s, a majority of American states enforced segregation through "Jim Crow laws also so-called after a black character in the minstrel show. Minstrel shows consisted of comic skits, variety acts, dancing and music, performed by white people in black faces. Minstrel shows portrayed Negro people as dim-witted, lazy, buffoonish, superstitious, happy-go-lucky and musical. After watching such shows all northern whites believed that all Negro were backward, indolent, immoral and unable to govern themselves, American whites insisted that Anglo-Saxons had to bring civilization to them. Also, whites often characterized such people as coons, mongrels, unwholesome, childlike, ignorant, lazy, savage and superstitious. Therefore, White Anglo-Saxon Protestants insisted that it was their responsibility to indoctrinate Blacks with civility through Christianity.

Racial inequality was not unique to the South. It was the norm across the nation, and other regions of the United States saw similar violence and state-sanctioned discrimination. Though Jim Crow and its specific laws and practices occurred in the South, the system thrived because it was sanctioned by the national government. The actions or, more frequently, inactions of the three branches of the federal government were essential in defining the lifespan of Jim Crow. Every state had different Jim Crow laws for their many different institutions and facilities. Here is a general list of the segregation laws.

- Nurses: no white nurse shall service in Negro wards or rooms which Negro men are in.
- Buses: All Negro's sat in the back and enter through the back.
- Railroads: separated departments for Negro and whites
- Restaurants: it shall be unlawful to serve both races in the same room.
- Education: schools for white children and for Negro children shall be conducted separately.
- Juvenile delinquents: separated buildings, white boys and Negro boys in any manner associated with each other.
- Intermarriage: the marriages between a white and a Negro shall be null and void.
- Barbers: no color barber shall serve white people be it man, woman or girls.
- Burial: the officer shall not bury a colored person on the same burial ground of whites.

- Housing: Any person. who shall rent any part of any such building to a Negro person or a Negro family when such building is already in whole or in part in occupancy by a white person or white family, or vice versa when the building is in occupancy by a Negro person or Negro family, shall be guilty of a misdemeanor and on convictions thereof shall be punished by a fine of not less than twenty-five ($25) nor more than one hundred ($100.00) dollars or be imprisoned not less than 10, or more than 60 days, or both such fine and imprisonment in the discretion of the court.

- Parks: It shall be unlawful for colored people to frequent any park owned or maintained by the city for the benefit, use and enjoyment of white persons. And unlawful for any white person to frequent any park owned or maintained by the city for the use and benefit of colored persons. (Georgia)

  - Wine and beer: if licensed to sell liquor must sell exclusively to one race only.
  - The blind: the board of trustees shall maintain a separate building for each race.

- Amateur Baseball: IT shall be unlawful for any amateur white baseball team to play baseball on any vacant lot or baseball diamond within two blocks of a playground devoted to the Negro race, and it shall be unlawful for any amateur colored baseball team to play baseball in any vacant lot or baseball diamond within two blocks of any playground devoted to the white race. (Georgia)

  - Hospitals: separated entrances for white and colored patients and visitors.
  - Prisons: the warden shall see that white convicts shall have separated both eating and sleeping.

- Telephone booths: the corporation commission to maintain separated booths for white and colored patrons.
- Lunch counters: shall not serve both races in the same counter, same room or same table.
- Libraries: the county free libraries but separate branches for each race.
- Child Custody: It shall be unlawful for any parent, relative, or other white people in this State, having the control or custody of any white child, by right or guardianship, natural or acquired, or otherwise, to dispose of, give or surrender such white child permanently into the custody, control, maintenance, or support of a Negro.
- Theaters: all public halls, theaters and opera houses shall be set apart in colors on the balcony.
- Military: the white and colored militia shall be separately enrolled, service and under the command of a white officer.
- Promotion of Equality: Any person. who shall be guilty of printing, publishing or circulating printed, typewritten or written matter urging or presenting for public acceptance or general information, arguments or suggestions in favor of social equality or of intermarriage between whites and Negroes, shall be guilty of a

misdemeanor and subject to fine or imprisonment not exceeding five hundred ($500.00) dollars or imprisonment not exceeding six (6) months or both. (Mississippi) Intermarriage: The marriage of a white person with a Negro or mulatto, or the person who shall have one-eighth or more of Negro blood shall be unlawful and void. (Mississippi)

The following Jim Crow etiquette norms show how inclusive and pervasive these norms were:

a. A black male could not offer his hand (to shake hand) with a white male.
b. Blacks and whites could not eat together.
c. Under no circumstance was a black male to offer to light the cigarette of a white female.
d. Blacks were not allowed to show public affection toward one another in public.
e. Jim Crow etiquette prescribed that blacks were introduced to white.
f. Whites did not use courtesy titles of respect when referring to black, although Blacks had to use courtesy titles when referring to whites.
g. White motorists had the right-of-way at all intersections.

Some simple rules that blacks were supposed to observe in conversing with whites:

1. Never assert or even intimate that a white person is lying.
2. Never impute dishonorable intentions to a white person.
3. Never suggest that a white person is from an inferior class.
4. Never curse a white person.
5. Never laugh derisively at a white person.
6. Never comment upon the appearance of a white female.

Jim Crow Laws[15]

Treating Blacks as inferior beings were the impetus for the government's many forms of segregation. Public services that were provided to black people were inferior to those that white people received. Furthermore, every Negro man had to have a job, or he risked arrest and enslavement as a free laborer for a big corporation.

The most institutionally racist institution in the public and private sector was the Christian Church. Understand that there was absolutely no need for the racist legislators to write a Jim Crow law for the Church because all the racism, bigotry, discrimination, and criminals came from the white Christian Church. Discrimination by white Christians was often the catalyst for the creation of various denominations of Christianity by Blacks who chose to practice the religion of their former masters. One Negro man tried to enter or join a

---

[15] Internet: sju.edu

segregated Methodist Church and was turned refused entry. Rejected from "God's House", Richard Allen founded his own church, the "African Methodist Episcopal Church." It was understood by Blacks not to dare enter a white church on Sunday.

The loss of talent, oppression and everyday public humiliation as soon as Negro people awaken and walk out his front door. No one knows what his day will give him. In general, the Negro people had to go to work, to school, do chores and do business matter if they had to interact with the white racist public and the fear of the unknown outcome. To live in a country where the white public service people inflict hatred on the darker race, injustice in the courtroom, and discrimination in workplaces and in the society all-cause psychological and emotional oppression.

Another example of white Christian domination was the latent form of slavery that was maintained under 'the guise of peonage' and forced labor from 1863 to the 1960s. The sharecropper syndrome or labor control that relies on debts ends results in servitude and slavery, however, outlawed in 1867 never enforced lay dormant for many years. The feudal system of sharecropping relied on the perpetual accumulation of debt from sharecropper to landowner. Racial subjugation on the chain gang victimized Negro men who were treated with barbarous inhumanity; underfed, lodged in poor conditions, and had insufficient sleep. They were often made to wear iron collars armed with prongs around their necks and gags in their mouths for hours or days. Prisoners were forced to drag heavy chains and weights while working in the coal mines, fields, and work camps. They were to strip naked, exposing their backs and limbs so that they could be cut with knives, bruised and mangled by hundreds of blows with brooms, whips and wooden 2 by 4s.

Despite the trauma that ensued emancipation, Blacks managed to develop themselves as talented and gifted musicians, entertainers, athletes, agriculturalists, business entrepreneurs and educators. Despite their strengths, the Negro people received less money for all services, resources and talents in comparison to their white counterparts. Throughout the Jim Crow Era, the Negro lived as second-class citizens with a third-world lifestyle of oppression, humiliation and absolute domination. After the Jim Crow Era, the white race continued to control and dominate the government, the business world and the whole of society. Sadly, the Negro people never achieved their full potential in any field of discipline because whites totally destroyed Black culture at the roots. Even though the Negro people had lost their sense of African culture and customs, they managed to establish a culture that was inspired by their history in America. Spirituality was one discipline during and after Jim Crow that allowed for Black to lead themselves. Within the Black church, white domination and persuasion were used to manipulate Blacks while giving them the freedom to explore Christianity and interpret the bible based on their experience as a people. There were many churches in the Black community and most were open once a week for service. The Black church was one beneficial business in the black community; however, there were a limited and scarce amount of Black boutiques, ethnic shops and companies that survived the Jim Crow era.

With the absolute dominance that racial extremist Christians had over the Black Christians, there was no need for the covert terrorist organization the KKK. There were many overt public humiliations, intimidations, and injustices that were with protection by law enforcement, Mayors and legislators. The same people who held these positions were the people who wore white sheets over their faces and bodies when they set out on missions to destroy property and murder people at night.

Every court case concerning Negro's after 1877, ruled in favor of white supremacy. The northern communication media newspapers, magazines and plays justified the southern oppression of the Negro people. They voiced approval of lynching and generally showed that Negros were so stupid and morally degraded that they deserved an inferior place in society. Between 1882 and 1900 there were over 3,011 lynchings in the USA mostly in the southern states by the KKK. The Klan grew quickly and became a powerful terrorist organization. It attracted former Civil War generals such as Nathan Bedford Forrest, the famed cavalry commander whose soldiers murdered captured black troops at Fort Pillow. The Klan spread beyond Tennessee to every state in the South and included mayors, judges, senators, church people sheriffs and common criminals as members.

100 years of Jim Crow starting with the republican (19th) President Rutherford B. Hayes and ended with a reluctant segregationist Democratic (36th) President Lyndon B. Johnson in 1965 with the passing of one sacred bill "the Civil Rights Act." Seventeen white Christians mostly protestant presidents support the Jim Crow laws, supported the KKK, and supported the everyday murdering of the Black Christian citizens of the USA. During the early years of the Wilson administration (1913-1917), the Democratic Representatives submitted more racist legislation than had been introduced to any previous Congress. Disenfranchised and demoralized, few blacks voted during these years, leading to an even greater indifference of both parties to the black vote. The Republicans did not need black votes to control Congress, and Democrats did not care about a black constituency. Had the Black Christian people been of a non-white-Christian faith example Islam, the United States Government would have used the US army (cavalry) to absolutely ethnic cleanse every Black soul from the soil of America? The Native Americans were the perfect example of a different race that retaliated in defense of their culture and beliefs and as a result, they lost all of their lands, their people, tribal rights and freedoms. Pure white Christian domination when will it end?

The greatest destruction to the Black African race of people first, the submissiveness to the white race through enslavement, secondly, Christianity a 100% white man's religion, thirdly education white people control what is being taught and what should be learned the end result is a 100% brainwash creatures. The first acculturation was being chained on the European sailboats. The second acculturation was landing in the new world seeing brick houses, different food and many white people. The worse acculturation was becoming a Christian (seeing a white god) however but still being a slave. The end result of acculturation was the stereotype of Sambo, a submissive half-man, half-child. This creature was an extreme disgrace to the Black race and again because of physical acculturation, brainwashing of the mind and worst white Christianity the destruction of the soul furthermore these factors continue today in the Black Christian world in America and in Africa.

Perfect examples are the black men who fought all the US white man's wars, the Buffalo Soldier killing the Native American (Indians) when he was a slave and after the war (1812) he remained a slave, during the first and second World Wars and Vietnam if he came back alive he could not get a job. With the destruction of black civilization, there were masses of animosity in the Black community, the first reason was capitalism example one, a person educated with good-paying jobs belittles the others ignorant and poor, also the many social classes from rich to poor, many rivalries, bad leadership in the black community, broken families and no good spiritual direction or guidance in the black church. In the field of justice if a Black person is accused of a crime tried by a white judge or an all-white jury of peers they were always be found guilty. Whites were rarely apprehended, tried or convicted of offense crimes against Black people. As long as it could be argued that the state was not culpable segregation and discrimination went unpunished by the courts.

The Black people in the 50s and '60s paved the way for other immigrants from Africa, the Middle East and Asia to come into this country with less discrimination, less racism, and less white supremacy. The black race forced the racist white Christians to act like human beings by challenging the government's practice and enforcement of its written laws that state, "we the people." Whites had to be forced to examine their policies based on the concrete meaning of this phrase. Every issue of desegregation served only to render more painful, heightened apprehension and opinion of the cruelty of the white bigot Christians. Abuse, torture and insanity from the state government, the school board, and the white racist society were seen in the case of The Little Rock Nine. The US Supreme (1955) Court decision of Brown v. Board of education established that segregation in schools was unconstitutional. These nine students who were America's models for integration had to be escorted to their Little Rock high school in Arkansas by the US army. Furthermore, the parents of these nine students forced their children to accept the responsibility of changing white Christian behavior and thinking. The governor of Arkansas initially prevented the students from attending the all-white school, but President Eisenhower overrode the rights of the state.

Civil rights include the ensuring of peoples' physical and mental integrity, life and safety; protection from discrimination on grounds such as physical or mental disability, gender, religion, race, national origin, age, status as a member of the uniformed services, sexual orientation or gender identity, and individual rights such as privacy the freedoms of thought and conscience speech and expression, religion, the press and movement.[16]

Political rights include natural justice (procedural fairness) in law, such as the rights of the accused, including the rights to a fair trial, and due process; the right to seek redress or a legal remedy; and rights to participation in civil society and politics such as freedom of association the right to assemble, the right to petition the right of self-defense and the right to vote.

Affirmative Action was first created by John F. Kennedy in 1961 to stop discrimination in government employment based on race, creed, color or national origin. Surely the white dominating Christians had a great advantage over their Black competitors in the job market and in higher education. The second executive order by L. B. Johnson in 1965, promoted full equal employment opportunity that forced the private sector to hire Black folks. White business owners complied by hiring one. If you ask these retired black men today if they benefitted

---

[16] Internet: Wikipedia.org

from affirmative action because they were the sole black man in an all-white company, they will hesitate before answering. If you ask them if the government or the state should continue with affirmative action, they will all say, "NO." These are just some examples of the brainwashed black men of today. Surely, without affirmative action black people would not have received jobs with the state, federal government or the civil service; not to mention the private sector. W. E. B. Dubois wrote in the "Philadelphia Negro," that in order to gain social mobility, blacks must leave the 'menial level' behind and move up socially. But, as history dictates, nothing comes without a fight.

The American people's representatives in Washington the so call representatives write legislation and laws with their pens one letter at a time. But what actually occurs out on the street according to these laws was a different story. The 13th amendment outlawed slavery, but with the 'guise of peonage' slavery remain in Southern states for a 100 years under Jim Crow laws and white supremacy/white Christian domination, the 14th amendment or the rights of citizenship and protection but with dominating white Christians intimidation, humiliation and KKK daily lynching all protected by the three white governments of the USA equals no protection, the 15th amendment or the right to vote again with states able to effectively disenfranchise African Americans therefore, no voting, no protection and no true freedom because of racist white Christians consisting of the peasants on the street, the policemen, businesses, state legislature and worse the people on Capitol Hill. In the early 1960s under the Kennedy administration, used the weak method of the phone to ask the many white racist governors to let the Black people vote, let the black students go to school, let the Black people integrate into public places and finally this very weak method and zero actions from the government in enforcing laws and legislations now over 100 years old.

It was so sad that the dark people from Africa lost their identity once they arrived in the new world. They were first called Negro and Nigger's by the hateful white dominating Christians, towards the end of Jim Crow they were called color people, next came the term African Americans. Lastly, the term "Blacks" came about because of two reasons, first, James Brown's song, "Say it loud I'm and proud," and secondly, to oppose the white race.

The culture of slavery was not a relic, it was still alive. Until this day, Blacks are systematically taught that they must always remain passive and subordinate to the master of American culture and Western Civilization: White European Christians. The Negro people had to fight for justice; fight for fair practices in the marketplace, fight for their individual liberties, and stop being oppressed and humiliated therefore riots. However many riots during the Jim Crow era were initiated by white supremacy and most casualties and losses were of the Negro people; 100% police brutality from white officers, no justices in the courtroom by white judges, discrimination at the workplace, being cheated when buying a car and buying a house by white salesmen and brokers again all by white racist Christian people. With education, understanding of the politic of the US government, the economic system, the justice system and still seeing discrimination on the street the only choice for the people were to fight which equals rioting and or fighting the white powers.

List of the riots that made a difference:

East St. Louis Riot 1917, Houston Riot 1917, Red Summer Riots of 1919, Rosewood massacre 1923, Florida

Tulsa race riots 1921, Harlem riot 1935, Detroit riot 1943, Zoot Suit Riots (Los Angeles) 1943

Philadelphia race riot 1964, Harlem riot 1964, Watts riot (Los Angeles) 1965

Long Hot Summer of 1967 in which 159 race riots erupted across the United States

The Orangeburg massacre, 1968 at South Carolina State University, Protests of 1968 because of the wars in South East Asia

1968: Nationwide riots following the assassination of Martin Luther King, Jr. 110 cities including Chicago and Baltimore were among the most affected.

1969: New York race riot, 1970: Augusta, Georgia may 11th race riot

1970: Jackson state college killing, 1971: Camden Riots

1978: Joe Campos Torres death, 1980: Miami Riots

1991: Crown Heights riot, New York City

1992: Los Angeles Riots or the Rodney King riots after all the criminal copes were acquitted.

2001: Cincinnati riots

Chapter XI

19th and 20th Century

The Muslims failed to defend the people
of color thought out the world
therefore the white destructive
Christians sailed to spilled blood, seize land
and incriminated the natives

Before the end of the colonization in the world of Africa, Asia and the Middle East, this was the finale of the European Christian domination over these innocent people of the world. The most damaging Christian secular empires were led by the British, followed by the French, Spanish and Portuguese. The British gave birth to the United States of America and became the most immoral of them all. Before the curtain was called on European Christian colonization in Africa, Asia and the Middle East, the mature conquerors invaded subjugated lands once again. With even better weaponry than before, the 20th Century European Christians shed blood on the stage of their conquest before making their grand exeunt. The worse oppression in the world is an ethnic group that was ruled and conquered by people that hate them, that changes their customs, and cultures (religion, language and lifestyles) but worse changes the laws and ordinances of everyday life than fines, punishes, imprisons and just ridicule and disgrace the people for life. Despite the fact that the British Empire's claim to fame cost millions of lives, they were proud of the land that was seized over the years and the riches that were accumulating.

The fast spiral disaster fall of the Ottoman Empire was attributed to the lack of intelligence, in regard to military specialties and the weakness in leadership of the other Muslim powers. The Ottoman Empire was spread thin, mesmerize in wars with Russia on the eastern front and engaged in battles with many different European countries from the west. To complicate matters, the Ottomans were also involved in a war with the Muslims in the Middle East (their only continued success).

By the end of the 18th century, all of North Africa was occupied by the Christian European dominating powers. One of the catastrophes against the Ottoman Empire was the Tripoli massacre in 1821 located in southern Greece. The entire Muslim and Jewish civilian population some 35,000 put to death plus 8,000 troops by the Christian Greek forces. At the mercy of Christian forces, the Muslims were wiped out. In 1821, in the Greek area of Navarino, the whole of the Turks population (3,000) were killed. The Ottoman Empire avenged their fallen comrades in 1822 when they slaughtered tens of thousands of Greeks on the island of Chinos.

Arab opinion varies in regards to the failure of the Ottoman Empire. The strongest arm of the Arab world, the Ottoman Empire did not provide support for the Muslim people outside of Turkey. The Arabs in the Middle East were left to fend for themselves when resisting aggressive Christian invasion and colonization. The Ottoman Empire could have provided the food and resources needed to manage daily life. Fed up with the self-absorbed Ottomans, the Arabian Arabs started a pan-Arab revolt against the Ottoman Empire to create a united Arab state in 1916. Although the Arab revolt failed after World War I, the sovereignty and control of the Ottoman Empire came to an end in Arabia.

The rise of the Saudi family was successful due to the help they received from the Ikhwan, the Wahhabist Bedouin tribe. Together, they seized Riyadh in Nejd and completed the conquest of the other territories that would become known as Saudi Arabia at the end of 1925. In January of 1926, Sultan Abdul-Aziz bin Saud declared himself King of the Hejaz and later king of Nejd.

The list below are some of the many countries that were colonized by the brutal white Christian European dominating forces, the name of the country, and the year it was colonized, the colonizer, the type of colony and the year of independence: [17]

Africa

Country	Year	Colonizer	Type	Independence
Angola	1575	Portuguese	Colony	1975
Bissau	1879	Portuguese	Colony	1973
Morocco	1912	France Spain	Protectorates	1956 1956
Mauritania	1904	France	colony	1960

[17] Internet: hobotraveler.com

Country	Year	Power	Type	Year
Libya	1911	Italy, France, British	Colony	1951
Fulani Empire (North Nigeria)	1903	France United Kingdom	Colony	1960
Swaziland	1902	United Kingdom	colony	1968
Ashanti (Ghana)	1900	United Kingdom	colony	1957
Burundi	1899	Germany	colony	1962
Benin	1897	France	colony	1960
Bunyoro (Uganda)	1897	United Kingdom	protectorate	1962
Congo	1908	Leopold II, Belgium	Colony	1960
Cameroon	1884	France	Colony	1960
Dahomey	1894	France	colony	1960
Gambia	1824	British	Colony	1965
Gabon	1885	France	Colony	1960
Guinea	1891	France	French Guinea	1957
Rwanda	1894	Germany	colony	1962
Rhodesia (Zimbabwe)	1890	British	Colony	1965
Oubanqui (Chad)	1894	France	colony	1960
Kenya	1806	British	Colony	1965
Ijebu (South Nigeria)	1892	United Kingdom	colony	1960

Bechunaland (Botswana)	1885	United Kingdom	colony	1966
Djibouti	1888	France	Colony	1977
Merina (Madagascar)	1885	France	Protectorate	1960
Mozambique	1569	Portuguese	Colony	1975
Mauritius	1810	British	Colony	1968
Namibia	1884	Germany	So. West Africa	1966
Egypt	1882	United Kingdom	British Egypt	1952
Eritrea	1890	Italian	Colony	1952
Zululand (South Africa)	1879	United Kingdom	colony	1910
Fante (Ivory Coast)	1874	France	colony	1960
Basutoland	1868	United Kingdom	colony	1964
Comoros	1843	France	colony	1975
Algeria	1830	France	colony	1962
Senegal	1890	France	colony	1960
Sierra Leone	1787	British	Colony	1961
Somali	1889	Italian	Colony	1960
Sudan	1898	British	colony	1956
Togo	1847	France, Germany	Togoland	1960

Tunisia	1880	France	Protectorate	1956
West Sahara	1884	Spanish	Colony	1976
Zanzibar	1503	Portugal	Colony	1963
(Tanzania)	1880	Germany, British	colony	1961

Middle East

Yemen	1839	British	Protectorates	1971
Cyprus	1878	British	Colony	1960
Kuwait	1899	British	Protectorate	1961
Oman	1839	British	Protectorate	1971
Palestine	1932	British	mandate	1946
Syria	1918	France	mandate	1944

Caribbean

Bahamas	1629	British	Colony	1973
Belize	1798	British	Colony	1981
Jamaica	1670	British	Colony	1962
Trinidad &Tobago	1802	British	Colony	1962

Southeast Asia

Malaysia	1824	British	Colony	1957
Indochina	1863	France	Colony gained	1954
Timor	1683	Portuguese	Colony	1976
Burma (Myanmar)	1886	British	Colony	1948
Cambodia	1863	France	Protectorate	1953

Laos	1893	France	colony	1953
Vietnam	1881	France	Colony	1945

South America

Guyana	1814	British	Colony	1966
Argentina	1536	Spain	Colony	1816
Brazil	1534	Portuguese	Colony	1824
Colombia	1525	Spain	Colony	1819
Peru	16th c	Spain	Colony	1821
Falklands	1833	British	Colony	Present
Tahiti	1880	France	Colony	Present
Venezuela	1522	Spain	Colony	1811

Asia

Hong Kong	1898	British	Territory	1997
India	1763	British	Colony gained	1948

The Americas, Australia, and South Africa were an exception to the rule. The Americas and Australia and the original inhabitants of these lands, the Native Americans (Indians) and the Aborigines, will never seize their country from the hands of their colonizers. These indigenous people will always be imprisoned mentally, spiritually and physically.

The history and demise of the natives all around the world were very sad and no one was to blame for this but white European Christians. The island of New Caledonia (named after a European explorer), first the slaughter of the people, then the diseases (Smallpox and measles), then the making the island a penal colony and bring 22,000 white criminals to the island and ultimately confining the people to reservations. Although Papua New Guinea gained independence from Australia in 1975, the country remains a British possession, just like the Solomon Islands of New Zealand which were also under British laws and the monarch.

North America

Country	Year	Colonizer	Type	Independence
Canada	1500	France	Colony	1763
	1763	British	federal	dominion
	Elizabeth II			
Mexico	1521	Spain	colony	1810

The British also colonized the USA or the thirteen colonies from 1607 to 1776

United States	1607	British	Colony	1776

Like its cousin, the USA started conquering, colonizing, and using capital greed as a motivator.

Alaska	1867	USA	territory	1959
Hawaii	1898	USA	territory	1959
Philippines	1898	USA	Colony	1946
Puerto Rico	1898	USA	territory	present

| Samoa | 1899 | USA | territory | present |

The Spanish–American War broke out on July 25, 1898. Puerto Rico was invaded by the United States with a landing at Guánica. Following the outcome of the war, Spain was forced to secede from Puerto Rico, and surrender control of Cuba, the Philippines, and Guam to the United States under the Treaty of Paris (1898). The American acquisition of the Philippines did not make life any easier for the inhabitants of these islands. The Moro Crater Massacre occurred between the belligerents, the Philippine Christian Constabulary and the USA Christian forces. Mostly unarmed Muslim Moro villagers including women and children (800-1,000) were slaughtered. These actions of military assault qualify the United States as an Empire with the politico-military dominion of the Philippine populations. Who are culturally and ethnically distinct from the (ruling) ethnic group and its culture? Like the British Empire's East India Company in India that ultimately seized the whole country similarly an American sugarcane company and businessmen practically did the same causing the annexation of Hawaii in 1898 also with help from the US government and the militiamen forces.

The greatest uprisings of native people against the white Christian oppressors were supported by the United Nations Charter of 1945 which grants "the right of self-determination of the people." Within only two decades the system of colonialism collapsed around the world. The UN may have been brilliant in the notion to pen the concept of self-determination into international law, but these countries had to physically fight for their independence. Many of the predominately populated Muslim countries like Nigeria were made to reform their constitution by the British and give Nigerian Christians most of the seats in the government. In addition, a Christian dictator was appointed which was the catalyst for civil war. Before British colonization, most countries were at peace, but when British rule came to an end, countrymen fought ferociously amongst each other, divided by allegiance to tribes, politics and religion. Hindus and Muslims in India, Christians and Muslims in Nigeria, and Jews and Muslims in Palestine continue to have political, economic, and social problems and feuds because of the malicious nature passed on to these once passive countries by the British (white Christian domination).

Mau Mau was started in 1952 in Kenya by rebel leader Dedan Kimathi; he wanted to revert back to his tribal original way of life before colonial British rule. However, he could not get the full support of his people mostly because of the psychological effect of acculturation, Christianization and their affinity for the sport of soccer and cricket.

In 1892 the British attacked the Ijebu (Nigeria) people in response to its barriers on trade routes between two cities Lagos and Ibadan. The British were successful and occupied the capital, burning the meeting hall of the Osugbo then they used their new mass weaponry the 'Nordenfeldt Machine gun mowing down several thousands of Nigerians. The Ijebu people were Muslims and their indigenous people's faiths were non-Christian at this time. Like the similarity of the millions of civilians in India, the British won the war, they used their trade method and they make all the money for themselves (The British Empire). Here we have the greatest eye-opener for the Black tribes of West Africa; the European government forces control the politics, steals their economy and resource, murder and slaughter them on the battlefield and worse the missionaries are there to convert them to the many white faiths.

The conquest of Algeria by the French was long and resulted in considerable bloodshed. A combination of violence and disease epidemics caused the indigenous Algerian population to decline by nearly one-third from 1830 to 1872. The same was true with the decolonization; Algeria was not regarded as a colony but rather a part of France. Algeria got its independence after several years of war (1954-1962) lots of rebellion from the Algerians, brutal, terror, military actions tactics and methods from France, after the death of hundreds of thousands of innocent citizens liberation finally succeeded.

Mohandas K. Gandhi very smart and intelligent man who realizes the advantage of conducting a peaceful resistance to the unholy, bloody, violent British Empire imperialist. By using tactics of non-violence Gandhi retook his country. Marcus Garvey a Jamaican journalist, with the emergence of Pan-Africanism gained strength in the early 20th century and demanded swift abolition of white

Christian European imperialism. Kwame Nkrumah who was inspired by the works of Garvey led Ghana to independence from the colonial savage powers, the British; also Gamal Nasser led Egypt to resist British occupation.

In April 1964, the republic merged with the mainland. This United Republic of Tanganyika and Zanzibar was soon renamed (as a) the United Republic of which Zanzibar remains a semi-autonomous region. A month later, the bloody, in which hundreds to thousands of Arabs and Indians were killed and thousands more expelled, led to the establishment of the People's Republic of Zanzibar and Pemba.

The Islamic situation particularly in Nigeria, Syria, Palestine and North Africa got worse before remedies and solutions were achieved. Such cases embraced a natural superior and inferior relationship between the races. Based on European naturalists' observations, whites gave rise to the perception that the anatomy of African women, especially the genitalia, resembled those of mandrills, baboons, and monkeys. This scientific claim relegated Africans to being evolutionary inferior. These claims are considered rightfully authoritarian, making European women superior. The white Christian race has perpetually made harsh critiques and exploits, yet black Christians love them enough to fight on their side, behave like them and mimic all things European.

The United Nations and decolonization: declaration on the granting of independence to colonial countries and peoples: adopted by general assembly resolution 1514 (xv) of 14 December 1960.

Refugees issues Somalia, Bangladesh, Rohingya ethnic of Burma, Afghanistan, and Sudan.

Today, the westernized Christian Africans and Asians laugh and make fun of the natives and pure indigenous people of their individual countries. An example of this self-hatred can be seen in the Baka people in Cameroon and the Massa people in Kenya. There were many colored people in the world; however, when they look in the mirror they ascribe to the aesthetic standard of white Europeans. There are many black Christian women in sub-Sahara West Africa that rub bleaching cream on their skin to make them lighter in hopes of becoming white. These are just some of the detrimental consequences of slavery, colonization, acculturation, assimilation, and Christianization imparted by the world's cruelest perpetrator: the white race. More research needs to be done to analyze the Black Christians in America in comparison with the black Christians in Africa. With this research, one can conclude who is more brainwashed and who loves the white race the most. However, a cure for this insanity is available, but most people are lost in the darkness brought on by white Christian domination. Unable to see the light, may God help them before it is too late.

Below is a general way of defining someone's race. The list of all the races and the ethnic origins that fit into that race from, "the Genealogy Book 2004:"

"WHITE **RACE**" - UK, Ireland, Germany, Poland, Belgium, Denmark, Netherlands, Russia, France, Northern Italy, Ukraine, Croatia, Czechoslovakia, Norway, Sweden, Finland, Iceland, Austria, Bosnia, Switzerland, Belarus, Romania, Lithuania, Hungary, Bulgaria, Slovakia, Latvia, Moldova

"LATINO **RACE**" - Mexico, Puerto Rico, Dominican Republic, Cuba, Bahamas Honduras, Nicaragua, Panama, Costa Rica, Belize, Guatemala, El Salvador, Aruba, Colombia, Venezuela, Ecuador, Peru, Brazil, Guyana, Bolivia, Chile, Paraguay, Uruguay, Argentina, Trinidad

"MEDITERRANEAN **RACE**" - Greece, Sicily, Southern Italy, Turkey, Egypt, Albania, Cyprus, Tunisia, Yugoslavia, Libya, Algeria, Palestine, Syria, Jordan, Armenia, Morocco, Spain, Portugal

"BLACK **RACE**" - Jamaica, Haiti, Barbados, South Africa, Kenya, Congo, Niger, Nigeria, Somalia, Ghana, Zimbabwe, Zambia, Ethiopia, Uganda, Botswana, Rwanda, Tanzania, Togo, [Mauritania, Mali, Senegal, Guinea, Sierra Leone, Liberia, Cameroon, Angola, Namibia]

"ASIAN **RACE**" - China, Japan, Philippines, Korea, Vietnam, Taiwan, Cambodia, Mongolia, Thailand, Laos, Malaysia, Guam, Hawaii

"MIDDLE-EASTERN **RACE**" - Saudi Arabia, Iraq, Iran, Qatar,

Kuwait, Yemen, Oman, Djibouti, Israel, Afghanistan, Pakistan, Turkmenistan, Uzbekistan, Kazakhstan, Tajikistan, Georgia, Azerbaijan, Lebanon, Eritrea,

The United Arab Emirates.

"OCEANIAN Race" - Australia, New Zealand, Indonesia...

India is not on this list and a couple of others too.

Chapter XII

The Arab and Muslim conflicts

The Arab Muslims are not shining. They need
The good leadership of Salahadin to bring Egypt
And Syria back to normalization, confidence
and discipline a stronger military to fight
the real enemy, because today there
is a new Crusade or Christian front the
US Empire and they are more vicious
than Popes, Kings of Europe and
their cousin the British Empire.

Islam itself was indeed coterminous with civilization, and beyond its borders, there were only barbarians and infidels. Christendom had certain special importance, in that it constituted the only serious rival to Islam as a world faith and a world power. But Muslim's view, the faith was superseded by the final Islamic revelation, and the power was being steadily overcome by the greater, divinely guided power of Islam. Christendom offered nothing but the darkness of barbarism from which there was nothing to learn or be imported, except slaves and raw materials. Islam created a world civilization, multi-ethnical, multiracial, international one might even say intercontinental.[18] But with strong religious rivalries (Sunni/Shia), a weak Caliph's, the Arab Muslims completely lost their status, the Ottoman Empire fell, the Muslims lost all respect, and dignity and the end result they have an incurable disease in their heartland. Today, it

---

[18] ibid

is unfortunate that Muslim's overwhelming desire to live in the opportunist Christian world.

White Christian domination still prevails. Look around and see the vestiges of imperialism, colonization and the development of the United Nations and their new world orders. Have the white powers changed the name of the game to International law? The antagonists of justice see vulnerable countries punished by rich nations and giant corporations who all project their powers across the world. The perfect example of this can be seen with the former president of Liberia, Charles Taylor. He was punished to the fullest extent of international law. However, a powerful nation like the USA instills confidence in the British and Israeli governments. The 43rd president received no legal consequence for launching the illegal war against Iraq and Afghanistan. This fits the Nuremberg tribunal's definition of a "crime of aggression," which they called "the supreme international crime." The charges on which, in an impartial system, George Bush, Tony Blair and their associates should have been investigated were far graver than those for which Taylor was found guilty. Over one million Iraqi people lost their lives because of a crime against humanity. White Christians commit atrocities and continue to get away with murder. There is no justice in the world but surely justice will come on the Day of Judgment.

At the turn of the 20th Century, the clash of cultures and the changing of the guard in Jerusalem's three dominating religions altered the fate of Palestine.

The Ottoman Empire, on the brink of collapse, still ruled over Palestine but the Arab Muslims' culture was under attack. In the mid-19th century, the Jerusalem residents started to build homes outside the walls of the city and the Jewish population began to increase. At the end of World War I and at the end of the Ottoman Empire's rule, the Christian British mandate took over. The 1917 Balfour Declaration Letter stated that the Jewish people were to have a homeland in the present area of Palestine. The Zionist Federation of Great Britain was established in 1899 to campaign for a permanent homeland for the Jewish people. This organization had tremendous support from more than 120 organizations and over 50,000 affiliate members. The second most powerful objective was the return to Jerusalem from all of the European countries. The Jewish people returned in fleets before the coming of the Jewish state or 1948. The Palestinians and the Arab people had no clue of what was going on. All of the Arab countries (Iraq, Syria, Jordan and Egypt) were under the British Mandate created by the League of Nations in 1920. They all had absolutely no political power, no economy and no military.

The next ten years consisted of Arab aggression and riots, Jewish immigration and the two-faced British who tried to keep the peace but instigated the Muslims to attack the Jewish people. The Jews received diplomatic support from the British and other European dominating powers. The Arabs refused to cooperate; therefore, the British suspended their constitution. In Turkey, Kemal

Ataturk a Young Turk overthrew the Ottoman Muslim rule. The Caliphate was officially abolished and Turkey became a secular state. Within the last 200 years, the Turkish Caliphate was extremely weak, they never gave good support to the Arabs, but instead, they oppressed them. All the Muslim countries were left to fend for themselves. As a result of the Ottoman dissolution, the white Christians dominated all of them.

In the next decade, the British mandate over Iraq was terminated, Abd al-Aziz Al Saud proclaimed the kingdom of Saudi Arabia, and World War II began. Adolf Hitler's Nazi Party of Germany gained support from Pope Pius XII and National Socialism was accepted by the people. Lastly, the Holocaust on the Jewish population occurred throughout Europe. The Holocaust was a German system of persecution and annihilation of Jewish people, with collaboration from 21 other countries between 1933 and 1945. Over 6 million Jews lost their lives. Where were the institution of the church and its moralities, and where were the Catholic Popes? The perpetrator of the holocaust may be the Nazi Party but at the end of the day, these people are Christians. The United States and Great Britain, as well as other nations outside of Nazi Europe, aimed to stop the German military and rescue the Jews. With the victory of the allied force in 1945, the Holocaust ended.

Although the British were diplomatically (Balfour Declaration), politically (Zionism) and military (train 10,000 Jews in the British army) helping the Jewish people throughout this wartime period; however in Jerusalem, the Jewish were the aggressor. They started an underground movement, a Jewish commonwealth in Palestine and organized a Jewish army. The end result the Jewish launched terrorist attacks against the British military, destroyed a power station, kidnapped British officers, and lastly carried out armed reprisals against the Arabs. The Irgun (Zionist paramilitary group) was building up overwhelming confidence they had an objective and Great Britain the most powerful dominating white Christian empire was in their way. They also knew they could easily gain victory over the Palestinians so they declared war against the British in 1946. Notwithstanding the British told the early Zionist Federation that the best way to receive a state was through violence. In 1947 the Jewish terrorist gangs went on a long terrorist street killing Arabs Muslim citizens, Arab villages, Government buildings, and British properties throughout Palestine. By January 1948, 721 Arabs, 408 Jews, 19 civilians and 12 British policemen had been killed and over 2000 wounded mostly Muslims. The United Nations proposes the establishment of Arab and Jewish states in the land but the Arab higher committee for Palestine rejects the UN partition plan. In 1947 the Jewish gangs, their paramilitary and Zionism organizations were inflicting criminal acts and terrorizing the whole state of Palestine murdering innocent mostly Muslims and some Christian worshipers; however, the United Nation an international organization, that stands for 'world peace' stated these criminal Jews should have a state.

The Palestinian Arab Muslims could not win battles against madmen's extremely aggressive Jewish (Haganah) forces in Jaffa on May 13, 1948. The following day the British mandate of Palestine ends and the declaration of Independence of the state of Israel begin. The more recently developed white Christian dominating power the reckless/ruthless USA immediately recognizes the *de facto*. Next, the surrounding Arab ancient countries of Syria, Jordan, Iraq, and Egypt were attacked but in 1948 these countries were babies. First, they were all under the Ottoman Empire for more than 500 years, next came the evil white Christian British mandates, then the Arab tribal people have to fight, dominate each other for leadership and pause from fighting to help their brethren. Again the Arab countries all have new political unstable rulers with weak, unorganized and not well-equipped militaries. The end resulted in an extreme disgrace and catastrophe to the Arab world and particularly the Palestinian people the Arab countries lost territory and worse over half a million Palestinians became refugees who fled to the West Bank, Gaza, and to the contiguous countries of Lebanon, Syria and Jordan. Lastly the good old US, Congress passes the Displaced Persons Act, authorizing 200,000 Jews only to enter the United States. The Arab and or the Muslim people need to reflect on history that the white dominating Christian powers of Europe and now the USA does not like the Islamic faith, its Muslim people and what it stands for.

It was 1948 and the Jews have a little state. Was

this blessing from God or was it the Wrath of God that they (the Chosen people) didn't have a state for 2000 years? All of the religious people in the world have a state, the Hindus (India), Buddha (China), Christians (mostly Europe) and Islam (mostly the Middle East and North Africa). The children of Israel came out of Egypt with the Prophet Moses and with help from God, they had to fight the Palestinians if they wanted the promised land but they chose not to so God gave them security, commendation and food for 40 years in the Sinai. Now the next generation of Prophet David was willed to fight and with help from God, David defeats Goliath and the Israelites have their state. Same people but the different times they have to fight for survival against Syria, Iraq (Babylon), Egypt and the Roman Empire but the difference was the Pagan Roman Empire which destroyed their temple and unstated them. In the early 20th century the Jews received help not from God but from the white Christian powers of Europe, particularly the British Empire. The British also told the Jews that they have to fight if they want a state. But with the Zionism federation, Jewish gangs and the terrorizing of the Palestinian, maybe in the eyes of God, these people will be punished on the day of judgment. On the other hand, the Quran says the Israelites will have a state. Are today's Jews and the Israelites of the past the same people? Lastly, the Ottoman Empire rescue the Jews during the Spanish Inquisition (1492), and send them to Turkey, Syria, Iraq, Palestine and Egypt where they lived freely to practice their faith, commerce and education.

The Jewish people lived with Muslims in Islamic countries now for thousands of years with no holocaust, no public humiliation and no force to convert to Islam.

After the death of charismatic Egyptian President Gamal Nasser (1970); Anwar Sadat became the next president. Dissatisfied with the level and quality of the Soviet Union's military equipment, and Moscow's (communist) quest for détente with the US, Sadat turns to Washington. The first country that recognized Israel as a state was the USA and the second country was the USSR. Know your enemy, know your history. It was apparent that there was a true disdain in the world for the Arabs and Muslims? In February 1973, Sadat sent his security adviser, Hafiz Ismail to the USA to talk with Richard Nixon and Henry Kissinger the discussions end unproductive. Ismail was also displeased reading a 'New York Times' report while flying home to Cairo that Nixon had decided to sell Israel 36 Skyhawk and 48 Phantom jets. The Watergate scandal, the Vietnam War and drinking on the job were just some of the issues more important than the Arab problems. The Arabs lost the next war the 6-day war on June 5, 1967, Syria lost land the Golan Heights, Egypt lost the Sinai Peninsula, Jordan lost the West Bank including East Jerusalem and also Israel captures the Gaza Strip. The fourth Arab-Israel War started on October 6, 1973, mostly Egypt and Syria against Israel supported by the United States, Jordan was not directly involved end result of Israel's tactical victory. In 1970 King Hussein and the Jordanian government help the Palestinian refugee people the most, however, the upsurge in the activity and number of Arab Palestinian paramilitary elements (fedayeen) within the state of Jordan threaten the rule of law and take over Jordan. King Hussein's armed forces target the fedayeen, open fighting erupted, and the end result was the expulsion of the Palestine Liberation Organization (PLO) from Jordan. This event is commonly known as Black September.

In the eyes of history, Menachem Begin was just as much a terrorist as Yasser Arafat; at the Camp David peace accord (1979) Egyptian President Anwar El Sadat represented the Palestinians. The three rulers from the Ibrahimic faith the Christian from the USA, President, Jimmy Carter, the Jew from Israel, Menachem Begin and the Muslims from Egypt, Anwar Sadat, the PLO leader Yasser Arafat were not invited. Jordan's King Hussein, Syria Al Assad, and the Saudis did not see any benefit in making peace with this new Jewish nation. The end result only benefited the Egyptians, they got their land back the Sinai Peninsula and 1 million dollars, the Palestinians had autonomy and self-governing in the West Bank and the Gaza Strip and the fate of Jerusalem was deliberately excluded from this agreement. At the end of the Camp David accord, the 31-year-old battling but surviving Israel state benefited mostly. Although they had less of a population and less land, they received more money than the Egyptians and new weaponry. The fact that the strongest of all the Arab countries signed the peace treaty, symbolized a separation between Egypt and Palestine.

Throughout the late '70s and the early '80s Yasser Arafat and the PLO continue to strike, attack, suicide bomb, and small battles within Jerusalem however, the Israelis won most of the conflicts.

In a violent world, violence earns respect in 1991 the Madrid Conference was hosted by Spain, and co-sponsored by the USA and USSR to start an international peace process and negotiations involving Israel and the Palestinians. The end results were talked about because the Israeli government does not respect any international bodies, and the UN resolution 242. Ronald Reagan even told them to stop building settlements, because they never abandon their expansionist policies. Yasser Arafat, the Chairman of the Palestine Liberation Organization and the Fatah Party, was viewed as a terrorist, politically corrupt and secretly amassing 1.3 million USD personal wealth but the Arab people view him as a freedom fighter who symbolized their national aspirations. In 1993 he was invited to Washington for the signing of the Oslo Accord ceremony with Bill Clinton and Yitzhak Rabin. The accords were only to stop the Israel Defense force from pointing their weapon of mass destruction at the Palestinian Muslim people in the Gaza Strip and the West Bank. This is all a game from the point of view of the dominating Christian world and it benefits Israel in the long term. The permanent issues such as positions on Jerusalem, Palestinian refugees (right of return), Israel settlements, security and borders were deliberately left to future negotiations.

Next, the Middle East Peace Summit at Camp David in July 2000, the host Bill Clinton, the guess Ehud Barak and Yasser Arafat. It was a complete failure. In a completely lop-sided negotiation, everything was in favor of Israel. First, Israel never obeyed the UN resolution 242, to stop the aggressive attack on the citizen in the Gaza Strip and the West Bank, to stop the settlement building in these same two areas, second, the Green Line in the border base on before the 1967 war, thirdly, East Jerusalem and the Masjid Al-Aqsa and the most important the right of return over half a million Palestinian still living in refugee camps in Lebanon, Syria and Jordan. Bill Clinton, the US government, the United Nations and the media that reports the news were the most unjust and biased people on the face of the earth. If you read the issues and the details a blind man could see that everything benefits Israel. At the end of the day, it was the Palestinians that were suffering in the Gaza and in the West Bank; they have to depend on Israel for everything: water, electricity, food, and medicine; they cannot travel, go to Jerusalem, or get help from friendly Muslim countries. The Jews have everything, arrogances, political power, powerful Christian friends the USA, the United Nations, and the British, who automatically support them with their powerful military and extremely sophisticated surveillance. Lastly, today's Jewish objective and scheme are to depopulate East Jerusalem of its Arab Muslim citizens, next to destroy the Dome of the Rock and or Masjid Al-Aqsa and this is supported by white Evangelist Christians of the USA the end results are based on their ignorance, Jesus will come. Maybe this will be good for the Muslim people of the world because the Muslims need spiritual help, social help, political help, and economic and military help. The Jews and the Christians need no divine help because they have weapons of mass destruction, political powers, economic power, media power, international bodies and friends that give support to their unjust causes. Jesus will destroy the anti-Christ, if an individual does not believe as Jesus believed then the individual is the anti-Christ. Jesus did not preach the trinity, nor practice the trinity, nor said, he was a god or the God, nor a son of God therefore this is all Blasphemy. The Jews and the Christians ought to accept Jesus the correct way this second time around if not they will be considered the anti-Christ and will also perish.

The Arab Muslim people have cancer in their nucleus and if they try to kill it, or destroy it, it will only expand so leave it alone. The Jewish state is now over 60 years old with enormous power. They are still supported by their Uncle Sam, and they have no respect for the United Nations. But in actuality, who does? Lastly, their surrounding neighbors are the most pitiful and disgraced people on the face of the earth. But what will these Jewish people's legacy be? Will they obey their book "the Bible", or obey the politics of the USA? History has proven that dominance prevails and once on top, no one wants to let go. They will follow the vain norms of the world until the end of time.

It is amazing that all of the ethnic Christian

churches and groups before the conquest by Arabian Muslims still exist in their respective countries; such as Lebanon (the Maronite Christians), Syria (the Greek Orthodox Church of Antioch), and Turkey which has different Christian sects. The Muslim Sultans and people that came after the fighting of the merciless Christian Crusaders still allowed Christian ethnic groups to live amongst them with no animosity or ethnic cleansing. Everyone had the freedom to practice one's faith and seek political power. After the fall of the Ottoman Empire and the end of the colonial powers, France gave their political powers to the Maronite Christians even though the Muslims were the majority. This multifaceted Lebanese Civil War started in 1975 and lasted 15 years. The fighting took place in the Muslims' backyard, causing the displacement of hundreds of thousands of Palestinian Muslims. The feud between the Muslim majority and the minority Christians resulted in the favor of the Lebanese Muslims or the Palestinians. If the shoe was on the other foot the Christians would be the majority and the government forces, while the Muslim minority. The Muslims would have experienced ethnic cleansing within five years after the start of the first war.

East of Turkey was Chechnya and Dagestan both federal subject republic of the Soviet Union, during the first Chechnyan wars fighting in the Caucasus Mountains, these white Muslims fought the Soviets during World War II, a victory for the Soviet Union. After the dissolution of the Soviet Union in 1991 Chechnya like other entities seceded from the USSR, except that Checheno-Ingushetia had previously been a division within Russia. So in 1994 the first Chechen war with Russia, despite overwhelming manpower, weaponry and air support the Russian forces were unable to establish effective permanent control over the mountainous area due to many successful Chechen guerilla raids. End result Russian President Boris Yeltsin declared a ceasefire in 1996, a signed peace treaty and Chechenya gained *de facto* independence as the Chechen Republic of Ichkeria. In 1999 Chechenya's economy was collapsing, the warlords had no intention to disband the militias and Aliyevich Maskhadov, the President of Chechnya his political fortunes began to wane. One bad decision after another were the people ready for Sharia Law and following behind Basayev (Islamist militants) and Ibn Al-Khattab (a Saudi born Muslim guerilla fighter) to invade the neighboring republic of Dagestan in support of the Shura of Dagestan separatist movement all causing the start of the second Chechnya war. The war ends September of 1999 with a major Russian victory, the retreat of the Islamic International Brigade and Chechnya was now again a republic of Russia.

West of turkey in the old Yugoslavia the last of the Ottoman Empire expansion and conversion of white European Muslims still exist. These white European Muslim people love their faith but the Serbia Orthodox Christians still have resentment from the 15th century of the first Ottoman Empire forces. First the territories of the former Yugoslavia before the fall of communism were

Bosnia and Herzegovina, Croatia, Slovenia, Kosovo, Serbia and Montenegro. Each province had a different objective and aim, the Slovenes who were over 95% Roman Catholic and wanted to be independent from Yugoslavia and stood their ground against the Serb aggression. Croatians were over 85% Roman Catholics they wanted to leave as a sovereign country they had a strong military army that held the Croatian territory and pushed back the forces of the JNA and the Serbians. The problem was the Serbians wanted all the provinces to remain under the Social Federal Republic of Yugoslavia.

Next was Bosnia and Herzegovina the people are 44% Muslims, 31% Orthodox Serbs and 17% Croats Roman Catholic, they passed a referendum for independence on February 29, 1992, but it was rejected by the inner forces of the Bosnian Serbs. The Bosnia Serbs had their own republic within Bosnia & Herzegovina, support from the Serbian government of Slobodan Milosevic and the Yugoslav People's army. Bosnia & Herzegovina had a Sunni Muslim president, Alija Izetbegovic and what would become a weak and divided military. The army of the republic of Bosnia and Herzegovina was largely composed of Muslims, the army of Republika Srpska mostly Orthodox Serbs and the Croats defense council army mostly Roman Catholics all fighting each other and defending their respective territory. The war was characterized by extreme bitterness, hatred of each other based on religion, aggressive fighting, indiscriminate shelling of cities, and towns, ethnic cleansing and systematic mass rape mostly led by Serb and Croat forces. Not like Slovenia and Croatia which had a mostly Christian population and strong and organized military forces, the Bosnia & Herzegovina Muslims were the weakest of the three and received the most civilian losses and casualties. In the siege of Sarajevo and the surrounding villages, the Serb forces surrounded the city and villages using weapons including artillery, mortars, tanks, antiaircraft guns, heavy machine guns, and multiple rocket launchers, rocket-launched aircraft bombs and sniper rifles. The Bosnian government defense forces inside the besieged city could not stop the blockage because they were poorly equipped and poorly trained. Again not like the Slovenia and Croatia that stood their ground the Bosnian people needed outside help and support, there was no Islamic Caliph, the Turks would not help and no non-Arab Muslims will ask the weak Arab countries for help. Next the Srebrenica massacre or genocide or ethnic cleansing of the Bosnia Muslims people, commanded by the general Ratko Mladic the Christian Serb forces went house to house taking all men and boys sent to a concentration camp where starvation, torture and mass murder took place.

The Secretary-General of the United Nations a white Christian statistics organization stated it was the worse crime on European soil since the Second World War probably more worse than the holocaust. When the United Nations finally did come to Sarajevo they told the Bosnia Muslims to give up their weapon and the UN will police the situation. The end results the Muslims gave up their weapons and this Christian organization called the UN watched and gave support to the Serb's continuation of the systematic ethnic cleansing of the Muslim population while in the west, the 42nd president of the USA the so-called free world was too busy having a sexual relationship with his intern and playing 'wag the dog.' If the persecuting people of the world have to wait for the United Nations a laid back New York-based biased organization to intervene, if European Muslim people have to wait for NATO another Christian based intergovernmental military organization to intervene and if the people being slaughtered and massacred have to wait for the man that lives at 1600 Pennsylvania Ave to finish his improper sexual relationships then there will be no justice in the world furthermore, the white Christians dominating powers should end and the UN should be dismantled. The war started to come to an end with the signing of the "Washington Agreement," a ceasefire between the Croatian Republic of Herzeg-Bosnia and the Republic of Bosnia and Herzegovina. NATO intervened in 1995, operating deliberate force, hitting the Serbian forces and positions from the sky and the UN continues to take statistics and support Christian Serb forces. The research placed the number of people killed at over 100,000 and the number of people displaced at over 2.2 million mostly Bosnia Muslims, making it the most devastating conflict in white Christian Europe since the end of the Holocaust. Lastly, an article reported in the New York Times on 7-10-2012, "8,000 thousand Bosnia Muslim buried in mark graves from the 1995 massacre from Christian Serbs."

The Sudanese Civil War first started in 1955 to 1972 here again now these black Arab Muslim people were the government, the majority but could not win the war against the malnutrition and starvation animist Christian people in the South. Because Islamic faith is God's religion and the Muslims try to put it into action. The faith allows the Christians, the Jews and any other non-Muslim group to be separate, govern themselves and also have economic power. It was these freedoms that many time backfires, on the Muslim majority population because they have politically incorrect leadership, their economy was always weak and undisciplined military, and then they want to fight and lose. In 1989 Sudan was seized in a bloodless coup d'état by colonel Omar al-Bashir and in 2011 South Sudan seceded from the North with the consent of Sudan.

The Arab political leaders act and behave like immature adolescents. They may be able to provide for themselves as individuals, but they are unable to adequately sustain a family. They are not responsible enough to take care of their family, their tribe, the economy, the military, and the everyday functioning of the government. Arab leaders were ill-equipped to make the right decisions for the betterment of their people. For instance, the 1990 invasion of Kuwait by Saddam Hussein was a cowardly act. If he had a strong military force at the time then he should have fought the Palestinian enemy. Why did he choose to fight a neighboring Muslim country?

Saddam claimed that Kuwait had been a part of the Ottoman Empire's province of Basra, which was rightfully Iraq's territory. He caused the start of the first Gulf War and Operation Desert Storm, a key event, that resulted in a decisive coalition victory. By virtue of Saddam's poor decision, Iraq's infrastructure was destroyed. Iraq withdrew from Kuwait and Emir Jaber III was restored to power in Kuwait. Saddam became the arch-enemy of the great white Christian powers. The Christian powers placed economic sanctions that only affected the Iraqi people, not the governmental staff, and thousands of innocent people lost their lives. It was not good to be an Arab ruler and live in a world with no white dominating Christians as your friends.

In 1995 a CIA agent by the name of Robert Baer came to Northern Iraq with a five-man team to work with the Kurdish leadership to plan a plot to assassinate Saddam Hussein. Pure white Christian domination that these people have the power to go any place in the world with malice in their blood cause murder and conflicts. Is this supported by the United Nations? The plan was to use 100 renegade Iraqi troops to kill Saddam Hussein as he passed over a bridge near Tikrit but it all fail because of communication problems. Unaccomplished Robert Baer and his team immediately left Iraq and returned to the USA where they were briefly investigated and cleared of all crimes. Shortly after the Americans' retreat, Saddam Hussein justifiably attacked the Northern Kurdish perpetrators and executed over 700 captured soldiers.

Surely, if any individual or group tried to assassinate a US president, the FBI, or CIA will first murder the individual, then his family, followed by his organization. A perfect example is the Afghanistan War, the Afghan people have nothing to do with 911 but they are being murdered every day by white Christian forces because they hosted Osama bin Laden.

Imagine what would occur If Martin Luther King, the civil rights movement and the Southern Christian members during the sixties were communicating with the USSR and their KGB for support with the task of civil rights and or interested in being a communist. Lyndon B. Johnson, the FBI, and the KKK would have justifiably ethnic cleansed thousands of Negro people from the soil of the USA. Furthermore, there would be no civil rights, no freedom to vote, no justice in the courtrooms and the continuation of discrimination and segregation would be a permanent fixture in the American lifestyle. Also, the US government during the J. F. Kennedy administration used the CIA and pay mafia criminals to assassinate Fidel Castro, the Bay of Pigs became one of America's most infamous Cold War Blunders and failed missions.

In 1998, the United States and the United Kingdom started a four-day bombing campaign against Iraq, known as Operation Desert Fox. Here, Britain and America practiced using their new weaponry and technology on the innocent people of Iraq. The powerful Tomahawk cruise missile was tested in Iraq, as well as the B-1B, F-16s, and the British Royal Air Force introduced the Panavia Tornado

Strike Aircraft. All of these aircraft were successful in their objection to obliterating infrastructure and murdering Iraqi civilians.

The 2003 Invasion of Iraq was per witch-hunt, then slaughter massacre murder killing campaign of George Bush and Tony Blair. The media continues to say this war was based on false intelligence. Colin Powell, the secretary of state, first tried to get the support of the United Nations and abuse their preference again with the United Nations Security Council resolution because they (France, China, France, United States and the United Kingdom) were the victors of World War II. They were given greater world power over mostly Arab and African countries to start wars, give sanctions, murder at will and destroy economic trade. But this objective did not work and who respects the United Nations; can the UN put sanctions on the US, British, France or any white Christian European country? However many European countries protested the war, stating there was no evidence of weapons of mass destruction in Iraq and that invading the country was not justified in the context of UNMOVIC's report. George Bush did not like Saddam Hussein because he threatened his father. Richard Clark believes Bush took the office with a predetermined plan to invade Iraq. The catastrophic event of 9/11 simply triggered the spark that caused years of explosions in the Middle East. After 2 years in the war, over half a million innocent citizens were murdered by airstrikes and infantry. The two Islamic sects Sunni and Shia's fought amongst each other, while Arab, Kurdish and other tribes engaged in old rivalry battles. In 2005 the Central Intelligence Agency (CIA) released a report saying that no weapons of mass destruction had been found in Iraq. Should the United Nations punish the USA and the United Kingdom, put sanctions on them; or accuse George Bush and Tony Blair of genocide, atrocities, and war against humanity? Ideally, if the United Nations had a true purpose and power, the USA and United Kingdom would be punished with the placement of sanctions. Maybe because of the weak leadership of Kofi Annan, the Secretary-General of the United Nations from January 1, 1997, to December 31, 2006 nothing happened.

It was apparent that the United State and the United Kingdom have the most incredible sophisticated surveillance. They can easily find any human being that has a pulse, be he walking the earth, in the earth, in caves and flying over the earth. Saddam Hussein was found underground. The FBI and or the CIA could have taken 100 agents with 100 dollar bills each in 10 different areas of Iraq to bribe the citizens into revealing the whereabouts of Saddam. He would have been located without dropping one bomb. Being that the US military did not murder Saddam Hussein but gave him a court trial. They gave him justice but on the other hand, they were also responsible for the murder of close to a million people that were innocent bystanders of Saddam and this Gulf war. And we have white Christian domination when will it end.

The pride that the great white powers (United Nations Security Council Resolution) have instilled in themselves intensifies with time. Unaccountable, they were happy and proud that they can kill Muslims all over the world at random, without just cause. The white dominating Christians negate any liability for the F1, F12, warplanes and battleships in the Mediterranean Sea, the Arabian Sea, and the Indian Ocean when they were the ones who pointed missiles at innocent Arabs and Muslim families. The media deviously shows soldiers, famous athletes and advertisements that affirm their mission to fight for freedom. Please name one freedom that the people of Iraq and Afghanistan have taken from the American Christian/secular people.

The Arab people are like chickens without heads, running around in all directions. The politics of the Arab world have become confused. Should the Sharia or Islamic law be followed? Or should preference be given to Western ideals? Perhaps we should pursue the old customs of Arab culture. Surely Arab Muslim people do not practice Islamic Laws. They were forced to submit to Western sectarianism. The ruling family practices the old Arab culture or what was known as an autocracy. The ruler named King or President takes a top-down approach. First, he represented himself, followed by his family, then his tribe and maybe something will eventually trickle down to the people. The Arab people were very selfish, emotional and coarse. All of these rulers and their families were in rule at the time colonial rule ended. It is time for autocracy to come to an end. The Quran says, "God will not change the condition of the people until they change within themselves." Mohamed Bouazizi, the Tunisian street vendor who set himself on fire on December 17, 2010, died a martyr. His public suicide was the catalyst of the Tunisian Revolution and the expansive Arab Spring. Most importantly, he fulfilled the verse. Tunisian President, Zine El Abidine Ben Ali stepped down within one month, making the protest a success and inspiring other Arab countries to do the same. Although he is charged with money laundering and drug trafficking and was sentenced to 35 years *in absentia* in prison (June 20, 2011), he now lives in Saudi Arabia with his family and plenty of money from the Tunisian government.

Thank God for today's media, cell phones and the internet! The Egyptians heard the news and their revolution started the next month. The primary task was to overthrow the regime of the 30 years sitting President Hosni Mubarak. The protest started peacefully with the military closely watching but with the millions of protesters from a variety of socioeconomic and religious backgrounds violence soon came. Hosni Mubarak immediately took sick, while in his hospital bed in the courtroom on June 2, 2012, he was found guilty of complicity in the murders of the protestors and sentenced to life imprisonment. Mohammed Morsi is the new President of Egypt.

Next was Libya, the madman, Colonel Muammar Gaddafi (words from the late President Ronald Reagan) became the *de facto* ruler after he led a military coup that overthrew King Idris in 1969. Some say Gaddafi did a lot of good for Africa, his people and non-Libyan Africans. But he has been in office for over 42 years just too long. Gaddafi was also hated by the white Christian powers of Europe and the people on Capitol Hill. The white Christian organizations used their clout with the United Nations to freeze their assets, establish and enforce a no-fly zone over Libya and employ all necessary measures to prevent attacks on civilians. The National Transitional Council and the National Liberation Army (the rebels) were armed with weaponry and ammunition. Locked and loaded, there was no need for a ceasefire and Gaddafi was slain.

Lastly Syria, not like Gaddafi of Libya, Bashar Al-Assad was a likable murderer of his own people in the eyes of the Christian and Jewish world powers. First, Israel wants Assad to stay because Assad kept his word when it came to the Golan Heights, so if Israel likes an Arab ruler then mostly white people on Capitol Hill also will like him. Assad's father Hafez Al-Assad ruled Syria for 29 years under the Arab Socialist Ba'ath party and Bashar became president in 2000 when his father died. The same situations as the other Arab countries overthrow the regime and charged them with a crime. But the world was not just, thriving off of stability in the Middle East the world was eager to demonstrate extreme hate towards the Sunni Muslims. Bashar Assad (is from the tribe of Alawites), a Shia group who help the British against Sunni's early 20th century. At present, the Assad is still in power with support from Russia and the United Nations. The Obama administration has done nothing but talk. Assad received more ammunition from international bodies and now has used nuclear weaponry. Some result of the genocide was over 50,000 of his people mostly the Sunni Muslims and destroyed the infrastructure of many old cities and villages.

Where was the peacekeeping force of the United Nations? Why did the UN immediately go into Libya to declare sanctions and resolutions of the "no-fly zone, and to stop an attack on civilians? These so-called UN permanent members (China, France, Soviet Union, United Kingdom and the worst United States) do not represent peace. Particularly the US instigates and starts wars throughout the Islamic world from the 90s to 2010 over a million innocent Muslim civilians have lost their lives from US white soldiers and their ammunition. Where was Susan Rice, the Ambassador of the UN in the midst of Syria's conflict? Has she even taken the time to read the aim and objectives of the UN (to keep peace throughout the world)? If she got past the first chapter, entitled, "Purposes and Principles", she would understand that it was necessary to interfere in Assad's affairs. Unfortunately, she is a typical educated and brainwashed Black Christian woman. Obediently, she adhered to the directions of the white Christian powers that employed her. The United Nations with its many bodies and the racist bully five members can end this civil war within 24 hours.

The 2010 south Kyrgyzstan ethnic clashes between Kyrgyz and Uzbeks two Sunni Muslim groups now Muslims fighting Muslims.

In conclusion, the richest Arab country and the one closest to the Islamic faith have absolutely done very little for the Arab and Muslim people. Saudi Arabia is the most hated and disliked Arab Muslim country throughout the Middle East. With the millions of dollars they received from oil revenue, they can build housing in Northern Arabia for the hundreds of thousands of Arab Muslim refugees and place an emphasis on providing a settlement for the Palestinians. Of all the religions in the world, the Muslims suffer the most persecution from the UK and the USA, which are supported by the UN. There are presently over half a million Palestinian Muslims who are unwanted refugees in Jordan, Lebanon and Syria. Their future is unknown because they will never be able to return to their homes. Because of the American and British invasion of Iraq, accompanied by the contempt that they had for Saddam, Iraqis are also vulnerable refugees and internally displaced people. They now live in Jordan, Syria, Turkey and other parts of the region, in slums devoid of running water, heat, and food, with no assistance or legal rights. Although the US military's occupation of Iraq has ended, the country continues to face large-scale displacement and pressing humanitarian needs. Of course, the United Nations has been instructed to turn a blind eye to this inhumane travesty as well.

There were roughly 27.5 million internally displaced persons (IDP) worldwide. Of all the religious people in the world, the Muslims and or Islamic faith are the most persecuted people in the world. Starting in 1948 Palestine and the surrounding Arab Muslim countries lost that war; the end result was over 300,000 refugee Muslims losing their homes and land because of the Jews of Israel and the Christian weaponry of the USA, USSR, UK and the eyes of the United Nations. Within the last 20 years, the IDP statistics increase by millions because of a few factors, capitalism, mostly white Christian domination, the United Nations' five resolution members and wars which were the core of the USA sustainability program. The Azerbaijan Muslims 1992 lost war with the Armenians Christians backed by the USSR more Christian forces the end result 1 million Azerbaijan refugees and internally displaced persons. The invasion of Afghanistan by the US forces in a Christian and sectarian country caused over 200,000 innocent Muslim citizens to be refugees and IDPs. Burma now Myanmar a Buddhist country is ethnic cleansing its Muslim population which is supported by the Obama administration because of his visit to the country that was presently practicing the genocide. Iraq was another invasion by a Christian country the USA and UK on a defenseless Muslim country and or their people the end result in the murder of over 500,000 innocent civilians, over 2.5 million IDP, the start of tribal war and the start of religious sect wars. The worse persecution of the Muslim people is present-day Syria and or Assad a Shia Muslim ruler murdering his Sunni Muslim population with over a million IDPs but most backed by and support from Israel, the United States and the United Nation. Furthermore, countries in Africa Chad, Congo, Ethiopia, Eritrea, Uganda, Somalia, Kenya, Sudan, and Zimbabwe are having war conflicts resulting in thousands of large populations of IDP while the United Nations watch and take statistical notes.

The Christian and Jewish media continue to make negative movies about the Islamic Prophet because they have freedom of the press. However, freedom of the press does not grant them the right to disrespect the Muslim World. This is highly problematic. The Christian people, the media and the President of the USA all show strong hatred towards the Arab people and the Islamic faith. There is strong white Christian domination in the Middle East and the Muslim people are forced to comply with their evil demands. The Obama administration is presently murdering and killing many Muslim people using air drone attacks. The confidence and the arrogance of the Obama administration prove that America can go into the Middle East to seek revenge and kill at will. When white Christian people and their government commits murder it is not considered terror or even sinful. The bible says to love thou enemy but the Christian people and government throughout history never fulfilled this verse. Lastly, Christian people do not understand spirituality, work and practical faith. We Muslims pray 5 times a day, we mention our Prophet in our prayer many times, and this causes us to have a very strong reverence for our Prophet.

In retrospect looking at pictures and old movies of the old Arab world, the visual representation of how the men were dressed was much different than today. In the

16th century Suleiman the Magnificent often appears in photographs with a turban on his head that consisted of more material than was worn on his body. In general, the Muslims from the wealthy merchant to the poor beggar was distinguished from the Christians and the Jews. The Quran instructs Muslims too, "Distinguish yourself from the Jews and the Christians." This distinction continues during the invasions and colonization period but good ethnic codes can change quickly. After the white dominating powers ceded control, Muslim men still wore turbans, but with less material. Some wore a fez, then came kufi's and thobe dresses. After colonization and during the 1960s, most Arab people, North Africans and even South East Asians underwent the process of becoming westernized. This change encouraged Muslim men to wear shirts, blue jeans and baseball caps. The true Muslims are the women because they still dress in traditional Islamic garb. An individual can see her in a crowd and identify her as a Muslim. Therefore she gets the Baraka's which are the blessings.

The Arab league was an extremely weak organization. This organization is unable to see the forest for the trees. First, the Arab people will always be tribal and politically incorrect. Second, the initiation of the Arab Spring occurred because of economic problems throughout the Arab world. When examining Arab politics or Arab rulers, all of the Arab countries have one man as a ruler and he has absolute power and all of the country's wealth. The Arab League failed to see that it was the Arab political systems that cause them to have no respect, no dignity, and no recognition. Furthermore, all of this causes them to lose wars that cause the Arab people to suffer. The little country of Israel that resides in the Middle East has more respect, dignity and military power than all of the Arab countries combined. After the invasion of Iraq by the new and old crusaders, the USA and UK, the Arab League should have declared war on them. However, the Arab League has no military and they were up to their necks in tribal and inner-religious warfare. The world is extremely violent with white Christian aggression. The Arab league watched as the US invaded Iraq and they were currently experiencing even more instability with the Syrian crisis. Finally, the Arab people need to see that the United Nations, United States, Great Britain, and Israel all want to depopulate the Arabs and destroy the Islamic faith beginning with the heartland of the Middle East. The white Christians will continue to strengthen their alignment and destroy one country at a time. Two countries are down, Iraq and Afghanistan, who will fall next?

The US and Britain stand behind Israel's onslaught on Gaza. Justice requires a change in the balance of forces on the ground. The Obama administration must account to congress for targeted assassinations of Muslim citizens. The White House will not even release legal advice about its drone killing policy. The so-call we the people thousands of secrets, planning, aggression, targeting the people in the Middle-east, do the people know what's going on. The website Wikileaks gave up some powerful information, truths, facts and US secrets however, the government quickly shut the site down and Europe creatively charged the creator with false sex charges.

Chapter XIII

In the '60s and the '70s

The Bible is a book the people carry to church
It stays closed mostly like the corner churches
All behavior is learned
Where do the people get their ethics from
The church the media the government
Surely religious principles are all in the closet
And the practices of criminology are on the streets

The sixties was a very dynamic decade with the rise of a counterculture, social revolution, wars, assassinations, and the coming the end of colonization around the world. The Civil Rights Movement, most importantly, was a terminal period in this decade. In 1960 John F. Kennedy became the 35th President. He was the first Roman Catholic to be elected and he was popular with the Black community. The Cold War, the battle between capitalism and communism and ferocious fighting in Vietnam caused many Americans to come back home in black body bags. During the March on Washington for jobs and freedom on August 28, 1963, Martin Luther King stood in front of the Lincoln Memorial and delivered his historic "I Have a Dream," speech advocating for racial harmony. The 1965 passing of the Civil Rights Bill did not hinder the public violence in the south. Black people continued to be viciously attacked by white racist Christians with fire hoses and police dogs. They used normal general white public humiliation, along with threads and assaults because white racist Christian people did not want to relinquish power.

In the late sixties black people quickly began to

gain social mobility, they moved into white neighborhoods and into the suburbs. White racist Christian people continued to move elsewhere. African Americans started to get civil jobs, enter white colleges and organize Black Nationalist movements. There were some positive white Christian people that exist. The counterculture people wanted to rebel against the cultural norms of their parent's 40s and 50s generations. They smoked marijuana, grew their hair long, dressed colorfully, listened to hard rock music and strongly protested against the Vietnam War and capitalism. Even though black men became Mayors of mostly the inner-city in the 70s, the evil element of drugs attacked the black communities and caused great regression in the community.

Defense, defense, in need of defense! There is absolutely no defense in the African American Christian society. Who does every American obey? Of course, one must follow the directives of the legislation, the church, the media and or TV (Hollywood industry). Most white Christian people obey legislation first, followed by the media, Hollywood and finally, the Church. Black Christian people loosely obey the church. The media influenced Blacks for sure, Hollywood was favored and legislations were their last directives. In the 60s employment was high for blacks; full-time menial jobs were available, as well as some civil jobs. Most Black men smoked cigarettes and drank alcohol because the actors on the TV shows were drinking and smoking. There was a lot of premarital sex and adultery because the morning soap operas showed plenty of unfaithful couples. There were plenty of murders and killings in the Black community because the majority of the shows on TV were based on criminal elements. There were some people that listened to gospel music in the morning on the radio; however, on Monday through Saturday, the majority of Protestant Christian churches were closed. On the contrary, most liquor stores were open 12 or more hours every day, people bought illegal drugs at all hours and prostitution was a 24-hour business. The numbers racket and gambling in predominately black cities were rampant before the state-organized this lucrative business. There were many black social clubs for professions like postal workers, firefighters, and correctional officers. These men would go to their perspective clubs from 3 pm to 7 pm to drink, smoke and socialize after work. Then, they would go home and have arguments and fights with their wives, and then they would eat and sleep and repeat the same activities the next day. On Sunday, the church was comprised of women that made up 70% of the congregation, preachers wore expensive suits that they jumped around the pulpit in while shouting the Holy Ghost and entertaining the women. The women loved the highly emotional services because they increased their adrenaline. One must ask, did Jesus preach like this?

The Black Christian people who moved up socially were very aggressive in the 60s and 70s because of better job opportunities that afforded them the ability to own houses and cars. But evil soon closed in on the Black community. The church closed on weekdays leaving the Black community defenseless against the penetration of the evil element. The movement to improve race relations and the civil rights of blacks had been a dramatic saga of marches, protests, speeches and landmark legislation. The road toward equality was very bumpy and there was no leadership to provide direction a guiding in the darkness. There were very intelligent, smart, and brilliant minds and many black men were getting into politics, becoming city council members, and Mayors. Many black entertainers and athletes in the industries were competing and winning respectively. However, there was a powerful evil white Christian and organized ethnic group that successfully targeted black musicians. The first wave of attack was with drugs. The Black athletes followed the downtrodden path of the musicians in the late sixties when they started taking hard drugs. By the mid-'70s, the next generation had all experienced smoking marijuana. But worse, the church remained closed. Blacks needed a strong defense to stand against the evil that came into the community. According to a 60 Minutes report in the late 1970s, "LSD" (Lucy in the Sky with Diamonds), a very potent mood-changing chemical, came into the communities of whites and blacks (in the 1970s) across the country. 60 Minutes stated that the US government manufactured the acid at the local universities, and then a marketing team sold the highly hallucinogenic drug on the streets. The American people were guinea pigs for the government to practice their chemical warfare on their own people.

The people were far from morality, without a sense of the fear of God in their minds or souls. The people understood this irreligious and white Christian economic system of capitalism. If they had to cheat, lie, or steal to make a buck, they did just that. People watched many black and white TV shows of white businesspeople cheating the people so they mimic what was seen on TV. Every family had a big console TV in their living room, maybe a 13-inch in the kitchen, and some had TVs in every room of the house. It stayed on even though no one was watching. Crime movies with Humphrey Bogart, James Cagney, John Wayne and Edward G. Robinson were popular and it was a pastime to watch westerns all day. White cowboys who shot and killed anything and everything became an idealized image. Many people admired the lifestyle that TV shows promoted, one that included drinking alcohol and smoking cigarettes.

The TV was more than 99% white before the '60s and it still is today. In the late '60s, there was only one Black sitcom on the air, "Julia" starring the elegant singer and actress, Diahann Carroll. Things changed in the '70s with the good old "Blaxploitation" movies. More Black sitcoms debuted on TV with leading black men like Bill Crosby and Sidney Poitier. Although Hollywood will always be a white racist organization, they showed their true white violent Christian nature on TV shows and movies. The white race was an eyewitness to their acts of terrorism, humiliation and killing of Christian blacks at random. It was possible that some of the good white

Christian people started to feel a little sorrow for their variety of evil actions. It was a miserable ordeal that every movie about the Jim Crow era has to show a black man being lynched by a mob of white racist Christian people. Finally, in the TV show "Julia", a single Black woman who raised her child alone would become the norm in the black community.

In the 60s we must talk about the violent nature of white Christian people, the Vietnam War, a war based on two competing economic systems. The Vietnam War was a war of arrogance where the 190lbs, six-foot-tall white Christian male fought against a skinny, 90lbs five-foot-tall Vietnamese Buddhist man. It was said that the weapon that the Vietcong carried and used was bigger than him. Many black men were drafted into this war and lost their lives for white Christian capitalism. The men that returned home could not obtain decent employment in this white Christian society, however, hard drugs, liquor stores and churches on the corner were always available.

Medgar Evers served in World War II, came home to Jackson, Mississippi and applied to then a segregated University of Mississippi (law School). He was rejected, but still became a very active and strong leader in the NAACP and Civil Rights Movement. He investigated the murder of Emmett Till, which caused him to be a target of white supremacists. He was assassinated on the morning of June 12, 1963, in his driveway. President John F. Kennedy was assassinated in Texas, in 1963. Malcolm X, a brilliant speaker, Black Nationalist, and human rights activist was assassinated in New York City in 1965; he died a Sunni Muslim. DR. Martin L. King, a Baptist minister, civil rights activist, brilliant public speaker, and winner of the Nobel Peace Prize was assassinated in Tennessee, 1968. Robert Kennedy, the brother of John F. Kennedy, a Democratic senator and Civil Rights activist was assassinated in Los Angeles, in 1968. These men were not in the Vietnam War but they were at war within the United States. It was a war of hate, anger and rage in the inner city, where discrimination and unfairness were embedded in society.

The law of the land was who rules on the street, what was said in Washington stayed in Washington. The white supremacy, the KKK and their political power remain dominant in the south for approximately 30 or more years because no justice came to these victims. The FBI, a government organization, was aware of who committed assassinations but did nothing; therefore, they were just as criminally racist as the KKK. The horrible atrocities committed in the year 1963 and the four girls who were killed in the bombing of the 16th Street Baptist church, were perpetuated by George Wallace, "The Governor." In his prime, he was the most racist segregationist and extremely evil creature on earth. This man ran for president four times. Finally, justice came late for all, if not most of the victims of the 60's atrocities. Many of the KKK was never accused, charged, locked up, and or put in prison. A white supremacist could murder a Negro man and walk down City Street the next day; they could also go to the general store and talk as though nothing wrong was committed yesterday. This was the lifestyle of white Christian people, especially in the south. They did not want to relinquish control and again the domination was supported by all three branches of government.

In the mid-'70s many cities with a black population of 50 or more percent experienced the advent of a black man becoming the Mayor, with the exception of Tom Bradley of Los Angeles. Tom Bradley won with less than 15% of the black vote because he was a very likable man to the white race; they voted for him. Power is when the people are represented in all branches of government: municipal, state and federal. The white Christian race has support in the local city council, judges, the Mayor, state legislature, the Governor, state representatives, state senators and even the President. They have absolute power, better known as white supremacy. After the many elections of Black Mayors, these men did not reach the next level of political success; such as the Governor's office or being a Senator. In fact, they all ended their political careers as Mayors. Dismayed with some of the black leaders that came out of Martin Luther King's organization (American Civil Rights movement) had small political roles in the inner city and some became Mayors. They saw the hands-on white corruption in politics but ran from it. Particularly in Atlanta, Georgia and the many other southern majority-black city-states but one of the big six leaders remained strong to the finish. John R. Lewis is presently a U. S. House of Representatives who sees all the evil and white supremacy on Capitol Hill but continues to represent his people. Of all the friends of Martin Luther King, I'm sure Martin would be the proudest of John Lewis. In the '60s and the 70s, Black people were still conditioned to white people's persuasion and leadership even when it was racist. This conditioning called for black people to remain subordinate to whites. It is the black race that worked the menial jobs owned by white men and they were the main supporters of white businesses.

The white Protestant Christian terrorist organization, the KKK started after the Civil War in 1865 to oppose Reconstruction and they were successful. In 1963, after 98 years of murder, setting homes, churches, and businesses, on fire, a march on Washington, riots and the lynching of thousands of Negro people, they still exist. The US government has never labeled the Klan as a terrorist organization, nor have they ever dismantled or waged war against this group. Although this organization has experienced periods of decline, they still exist today.

Some well-known Black Nationalist organizations were the Moorish Science Temple, the Nation of Islam, the Black Panthers, the Move, and Marcus Garvey; who supported the Back to Africa and Rastafarian movements. The Move organization was founded in Philadelphia in 1972, by John Africa. The "Christian Movement for life's," objective was to return to a hunter-gatherer society. Members opposed science, medicine and technology. They lived in communal groups and frequently engaged in public demonstrations that attracted the Philadelphia police department. The people wore dreadlocks and harbored compost piles of garbage and human waste in their yards which attracted rats and cockroaches. In 1985 the police dropped a bomb on the Move's row houses from a helicopter. The explosion ignited a fire and the entire block of some 65 homes went up in flames. The fire department watched and the police department fired over 10,000 rounds. Ramona Africa and one child were the only two survivors.

The Black Panther Party started in Oakland, California 1966, by Huey Newton and Bobby Seale. This was a revolutionary socialist organization for the protection of African-American neighborhoods from police brutality and self-defense. The Panthers went beyond the local police. J. Edgar Hoover, a pure racist director of the FBI called the organization, "the greatest threat to the internal security of the country." He supervised an extensive program of surveillance, infiltration, perjury, police harassment, assassination, and many other tactics designed to undermine Panther leadership, incriminate party members and drain the organization of resources and manpower. Angela Davis alleges that federal, state and local enforcement went to great lengths to discredit and destroy the organization, including assassination. Also, J. Edgar Hoover made a statement to all the police departments across the country, "to give every black man a police record." Therefore, after job application and background check, there will be no job for the black men to take care of themselves and family.

The Moorish Science Temple is an American

religious organization founded in the early 1920s by Timothy Drew also known as Noble Drew Ali a (false prophet). His primary tenet is the belief that all African-Americans are of Moorish ancestry, specifically from Morocco and in their religious texts they adherent themselves as Asiatic. Mostly because of the white race that can trace their ancestry back to a particular country in Europe (England, Germany, France) Noble Drew Ali says all African-Americans are from the particular country of Morocco. In 1787 Morocco was the first nation to recognize the fledgling United States as an independent nation under Sultan Mohammed III. However, Noble Drew Ali makes a very weak claim that all African-Americans should be Moorish Americans. The Moorish dynasties were mostly in Morocco and Spain and ended in the latter part of the 15th century. A few Moorish dynasties did reach Senegal and North Nigeria but this was three hundred years or more before the start of the European Atlantic slave trade. The Atlantic slave trade took place from the 16th through to the 19th century and the slaves were taken from central and western parts of the continent absolutely not North Africa and or Morocco. Furthermore, Noble Drew Ali adhered to a greater weaker claim that all African-Americans descended from the ancient inhabitants of Moab which is in present-day Jordan. He couldn't prove to himself that he was Moorish-American or Moroccan or Asiatic let alone the thousands to millions of Negro in America during that time. And worse Noble Drew Ali and his entire follower are not Muslim because he called himself a prophet of Islam and those people following him both violated the Quran, "that Muhammad is the seal of the Prophets."

The Nation of Islam was not a religion although it uses the word Islam and the word Muslim. Elijah Muhammad born in 1897 in Georgia, aka Elijah Poole, was a clever salesman in Chicago before meeting Fard Muhammad who introduced him to Islam in the early 1930s. Fard Muhammad from New Zealand mixed-race one parent from Pakistan, disappearance in June 1934, therefore, Elijah Muhammad creates the Nation of Islam calling himself a messenger, not a Prophet and calling Fard Muhammed (Allah) but not God, again calling the followers Black Muslims, not Moslems which the British called the people in the Middle East. Based on Elijah Muhammad the Nation of Islam was the opposite of Christianity; Christianity has a tangible white God and a white Prophet now the Nation of Islam has a tangible black god, (Fard Muhammad) and a black prophet (Elijah Muhammad). Elijah Muhammad was a very clever man; he knew that the Negro's do not read most communication in the Negro community was word of mouth. If Malcolm X would have went to the library and read the 'Encyclopedia Britannica' it would have informed him about the truth of the Islamic faith. In order to gain converts, he used his salesmen tactics by asking about 25 questions that required a simple yes, followed by the last question that asked, "Do you want to convert?" Having said, yes 25 times, a yes was guaranteed as an answer for the 26th question. The Nation was very aggressive toward the Black community. Their biggest assets were two dynamic public speakers: Malcolm X and later, Louis Farrakhan. Male members of the Nation of Islam sold newspapers, and bean pies and owned restaurants. Their favorite statement was "the white man is the devil." Beyond this, they did nothing. Upon Elijah Muhammad's death in 1975, his son, Wallace (Warith) Deen Mohammed, shared with the members of the Nation of Islam that the whole movement was false. He said that his father was not a messenger and suggested that they all convert to real Islam and/or become Sunni Muslims and most did.

In retrospect, one can say that Martin Luther King and his Civil Rights Movement, along with his involvement with the President, his march on Washington and the passing of the 1965 Civil Rights Act, did more for the Black race than any other Black Nationalist group. But the Black Panther's ideology, philosophy, ethics and self-defense for the black people community had more longevity; but shallow faith in God was a part of the group's downfall. The problem in the Black community will always be the dominating matriarch, the black Christian woman who loves the church, and loves the white race even though what they represent was not good for the greater black race. The Nation of Islam and the Moorish Science temple was definitely the worse of the Black Nationalist groups because if people die under the name of a false prophet and false god many lives will be forsaken. Black Christian people who follow the practices and behaviors of the white Christians were a disaster in the making. Believe it or not, the black preacher learned his preaching style from white preachers. Being that blacks lost their African heritage and customs, they follow the examples, behaviors and socialization of the white race; along with the evil and criminal nature of the white race therefore no future hope!

Did the US government truly start out as a secular government? Because the founding white fathers wrote the US Constitution and the Bill of Rights with very short sentences, it was general and vague. The reality behind these documents was that black people from Africa began their lives in America as slaves; therefore the white people from Europe had a labor force to work for them. The natives were ethnically cleansed by the white Protestant Christian racist people because they stood in their way of absolute domination. The First Amendment that grants freedom of religion means that one must have faith in one of the white man-made Protestant denominations only. In the first hundred years of the United States, the white Christian people had an absolute preference, power, and supreme sovereignty over people, territories, economics and politics. They had the opportunity to get a good education, gain military power, received employment, and obtain economic growth and political power. This practical opportunist took advantage of all the preferential treatment that was given to him by the government. After slavery, the Negro people could fight wars for the white racist government but could not receive jobs and social growth; instead, they were given options of poverty and depression. The natives have been massacred and slaughtered from New York to California and their population became less than a million. Their land was taken away and their only friends were the white Christians and their faith, the white man's alcohol, drugs, cigarettes and diseases. The same was true in the Black community where the churches were closed and the people drink alcohol, use drugs, and engage in prostitution and black-on-black crimes. Finally, this white Christian government gave the Europeans preference to be unfair in the marketplace, no justice in the courtroom, the right to destroy property and commit murder with no accountability. There was no remedy or justice for the non-white people that live in the USA. Again, the government, judges, and legislators were all protestant Christian people that supported white Christian behavior even when it was unethical, immoral and against the bible. This is the truth of white Christian domination in full bloom.

The desire to deny certain persons the right to vote was not new. One major outcome of the civil war was the enactment of several Jim Crow laws mandating a separate but equal status for African Americans. Those Jim Crow laws, which included traditional voter suppression tactics such as poll taxes and literacy tests, were used to keep African Americans from participating in elections. It was not until 1965 and the passage of the Voting rights act which prohibits states from "imposing any voting qualification or prerequisite to voting or deny or abridge the right of any citizen of the United States to vote on account of race or color" that the United States sought to eradicate certain states long-standing role in voter suppression. What government was trumped the federal or the state? If the federal government passes the 13th, 14th, and 15 amendments strictly for the Negro people and the state countered with Jim Crow laws and on the street, the Negros people were forced to obey the Jim Crow laws then the state laws were trumped. [19]

In retrospect, even with the terribly adverse circumstances under which Negroes lived, the likelihood of Negro eradication in America is real. As survivors of three hundred years of prejudice, humiliation and discrimination, the Black populous is in immediate danger of extinction today. The church has a veil over its eyes and its mouth is sealed shut. The church's followers and supporters do whatever the legislators tell them to do. They even support big evils like same-sex marriages, abortion, drugs, crime and educated ignorant young people. There are many college graduates and young professionals of the opposite sex that have no intention of getting married or pro-creating. Today's generation between the ages of 16 and 35 are told by the media, Hollywood, legislators and the church to practice and experiment with same-sex courtship. They are urged to experience 'this,' today and to experience 'that' tomorrow. The black population is decreasing rapidly.

---

[19] Minority news:

During Obama's campaign for president and after he won the presidency, the white Christian race went out and purchased weaponry and more ammunition. Who shall they kill? Certainly, they must kill the black Christian race. For the Blacks who are impoverished, live in the inner city, and dwell in anger and ignorance, criminal acts will always continue to be waged against each other. There will continue to be a large population of Black people who murder and kill each other, and blacks will continue to shuffle in and out of the judicial system and become infected with HIV or AIDs. The future for this Christian society is bleak.

Freedoms in the USA are based on the legislations that tell people how to live, the media that determines right from wrong and the entertainment industry that dramatizes the freedom behavior, going to the extent of teaching people how to murder those you dislike. All of these influences are man-made. The people are told psychologically and subconsciously not to respect and obey God and to ignore God's Prophets and His books. There is a God in heaven and the people need to understand Him, know His religion, His objective, how to worship and how to accept the Prophets that came with God's messages. In this secular society, people are told to get a good education and a good job. People are urged to be individualists, chase materialism, buy guns and physically indulge in evil behavior. These norms dictate behaviors that are reinforced by the media, Hollywood, schools, churches and the government.

Reverend Dr. Martin Luther King stated in one of his powerful speeches, "I've Been to the Mountaintop," (delivered April 3, 1968, Mason Temple Church, Memphis, Tennessee) although he lived in the inner cities, he says, "I have seen the mountain top, and I've looked over, and I've seen the Promised Land, I may not get there with you, but I want you to know tonight we, as a people, will get to the promised land! This was such a beautiful metaphor. This was a man living in complete fear, he was under 24-hour's surveillance, he can sense death, can feel it, can taste it, smell it, and it was all around him. It's the worse feeling in the world to know that you are about to be assassinated. The FBI agents were in your midst, tampering with his food, drink, cigarettes, and writings. They constantly interfered with King's life and this drives a person insane because you don't see them, nor your friend or associate and if you explain what is happening your friend and associates will think you are crazy and or going crazy. This was just the start of white Christian surveillance manufactured by the US government attacking people all over the world when they hate an individual and they've intended to eliminate him from the face of the earth.

Some more awful behaviors, "Fads"

Should people change along with societal norms or should they hold on to faith, principles and morality? In this innovative, Christian secular society with media available 24 hours a day and a closed church, people will follow worldly evils. Some of the many fads that developed in the black community were followed with enthusiasm for a period of time, and the behaviors were perceived as a novel or the "in" thing. All of the Black entertainers of the 60s and their predecessors had straightened hair and the women wore wigs. Next came the gold tooth, crown tooth, in the late 60s elephant legs pant, the early 70s came the mini shirts and platform shoes. The music was changed from jazz in the '40s & '50s to rhythm and blues in the 60s and the 70s and the start of 80s disc-go music. It was imaging so many Black Christian people wanted to be like white people in the 60's more than 95% of black women brought their daughter's white doll babies and another sad reality these same black mother's sons that were entertainers and athletics quickly started sleeping, dating and marrying white women.

In the 80s giant expenses gold necklaces around the necks of men and women or the jewelry fads, the most famous Black man "Mr. T," you couldn't see his neck for the gold. In the 90 the growing of a tail at the nape of men's and boys' hair; was a trend. Also the following or seeing black basketball players therefore the piercing of both ears my men and worse the black mothers were destroying their son by piercing their young innocent boy's ears early in life.

In 2000 and the present day, homosexuality was in full bloom. This is the accepted norm in this dominating sinning Christian society we live in. Homosexuality was taught and practiced in the schools, on TV and on Sundays at church. Girls can be seen on the bus stop bench sitting on each other's laps, showing no shame in kissing. The bible says in Leviticus 20:13, "If a man lies with a male as with a woman, both of them have committed an abomination, they shall be put to death." But who obeys the bible today? Also, the display of sexual pleasure at three o'clock in the afternoon doesn't give a shy boy a chance in hell of getting a girlfriend. Tattoos and piercings all over the body were popular; in particular tongue piercings in the middle of the tongue by women stimulate the male sex organ, while piercing of the front tongue stimulates the female sex organ. Young men wear pants that rest below the buttocks and they proudly show everyone their underwear and the younger the guy was, the more butt the people will see. Another disgusting type of behavior seen on the street was homeless down on your luck lesbians who dress like the young men who expose their butts. Some are proud, drunken; drug-addicted looking like hobos of the 1930s.

One of the worse groups is the professional athletes who have tattoos that cover 90% of their upper body. Most wear two earrings and Mohawks' haircuts. These men are purely disgusting, setting a bad example for the youth who have no mentors, just a bling-bling lifestyle to observe and mimic. They apparently have not read the book of Leviticus and the verse, "Do not mark your skin with tattoos." These people may die as Christians but they do not live by the laws in the Old Testament.

Many of these fads encourage lifetime or permanent damage to the body. However, the truth is available, but the people choose to reject it because it is not shining and the people of the truth are victims of persecution all around the world. American society chases capitalism, individualism, and materialism like a wildebeest in search of water.

Finally, African Americans were conditional second-class citizens. They have completely lost their entire African heritage through acculturation, assimilation and the conversion to Christianity. They are what the white dominating Christian wants them to be. The economic status of Blacks does not matter because their brains are whitewashed. They have quickly learned and adopted all the dysfunctional behaviors of this Christian/secular society. Blacks know how to be a criminal; therefore the end result is that they provide the bodies to fill the jails and prison system.

Chapter XIV

Nature and World Politics

According to the Islamic faith
The birds the bees the flowers and
the seeds are all Muslims.
Merriam-Webster's definition of Muslim is
one who submits to God.
God gave mankind and or Adam
the trust and Adam chose free will.
However nature chose to be programmed to
obey God therefore all of nature are Muslims.

Lynn Townsend White was a professor of medieval history at Princeton and Stanford, but he ended his career at UCLA. His main research topic was the role of technological inventions in the middle ages. His historical research has led him to blame Medieval Western Christians for their psychic foundations of technological inventiveness, which attributed to the root cause of the ecological crisis in the 20th century. He claims in his article, "The Historical Roots of our Ecological Crisis'" that Christians inculcated a specifically exploitative attitude toward nature and consequently, Christianity bore a great burden of guilt for the current environmental crisis. Because Christianity was arrogant toward nature and views nature as having no reason for existence except to serve mankind, Christianity was guilty of crimes against nature. Even modern environmentalists and conservationists generally hold the view that Christian people were environmentally unfriendly. Although White should have gone a little deeper in his religious research, he would have made the distinction between what Muslims were doing in their environment and how they built, invented, and discovered in their golden age of technology. The Quran says the same, that man should utilize the earth as he pleases. The problem was that white-dominated pro-Christian people only see the Europeans or the Christian world where nobody else was worthy but the white man.

If looking at the Muslims from a religious perspective, particularly the Arabs, compared with the white Christians or the Europeans, the Muslims and the Arab people did dominate but did not practice abuse. The original Arab Muslims did dominate the Berbers, the Indians, the Africans and the European but they did not abuse, slaughter and massacre the people as did the Christians in their history. When the Arab Muslims converted the Berbers of North Africa, for example, it was the Berbers that stormed in and conquered Spain, although the Arabs were given the credit. The Islamic faith gave each and every ethnic group a sense of honor, dignity and well-being. Therefore these ethnic groups rose up and made a name for themselves in history. The Muslim people and their rulers did not abuse the earth, the air and the water compared to the white Christian people. For two generations of Arab exploration, Arab people sailed in the South Pacific in their little boats and only had the intention to conduct trade. The end result was that the mostly Buddhist people of Indonesia and Malaysia accepted Islam on the honesty, trustworthiness and good nature of these

Muslims without bloodshed or violence.

When the Arab Muslims conquered India and ruled it for hundreds of years, the Hindu people and the Muslim people had an understanding of how to live together in peace. The Muslims did not go into the jungle and kill large populations of animals or destroy nature. But when the white Christians (the British Empire) invaded the land they used capitalist values, reckless behaviors and weapons of mass destruction. First the British saw that India was ruled by their number one enemy, the Muslims; whom they hated from the many Crusades. Therefore, the superior weaponry, the mercilessness and evil arrogant Christians started wars that killed massacred and slaughtered thousands of Muslims and Hindu civilians. After conquering the country the white Christians immediately went out into the jungles of India and slaughtered large game: the tigers, the elephants and other animals lost their lives. The end result was that the Muslims and Hindus had to separate and thousands in these two groups lost their lives. The tigers and other large game became an endangered animals within a hundred years after the invasion of the barbarous white Christians. It may not be in the Quran but it is in the ethics of Islam that Muslims can go into the jungle and hunt a particular game for food; unlike the white Christians that killed for hate, sport and entertainment.

I truly agree with White's article in the long term but not in the short term. First, the Christian people, the Crusaders and their European kings learned, received, and stole much knowledge. They gained technology and information during the many Crusades from the Islamic world. Secondly, the Christian people, the kings, in particular, had every right to seek knowledge and better their lifestyle. Thirdly, I agree with the verse in the bible; "And God created man in His own image, in the image of God He created him; male and female he created them. And God blessed them; and God said to them, 'Be fruitful and multiply, and fill the earth, and subdue it; and rule over the fish of the sea and over the birds of the sky, and over every living thing that moves on the earth.'" The Quran says something similar, "That man should be a vicegerent on the earth." It does not say the Believers, or the Muslims but man, meaning all of mankind. The traditions from the Quran and the Prophets deem the environment as a sacred place. People can gain profound knowledge from nature; thus, God swears by nature many times in the Quran, informing us that human beings are to preserve nature and look after it. Furthermore, the Quran refers to the beauties of nature. It states that man cannot count the many resources that God has given him; thus man is God's representative on this planet, if he is not charged with sustaining it, then at least he must not destroy it.

There is a whole list of discoveries, technologies, and inventions that the Muslims of Spain received credit for. The Muslims in Syria had better or stronger steel or iron in which they made their swords, which were stronger than the swords used by Christians. History calls the medieval Christian era the "Medieval Ages" because the Christians were in the Dark Ages. However, the Muslims were in their Golden Age because of their beliefs, the practice of the belief, the marketplace, education and the overall ethical lifestyle of the people. The Christians were on the bottom during the Medieval Period, but after many wars with the Muslims, traveling the seas and war with each other, they opened their eyes. The Christians always had better ships to sail the seas, and when the European Renaissance came about advancements were made in inventions, discoveries, and technologies. By the 16th and 17th Centuries, the Christians were much more advanced than the Muslims. During this period of history, the Muslims felt that they could not learn anything from the Christians or an infidel people. Even though the Prophet said, "Seek knowledge even if you have to go to China," the seeking of knowledge meant learning a profession and or a skill but not religious knowledge. However, the Muslims did not visit Christian countries to learn or to be inquisitive. Perhaps it was because they did not trust the Christians because of all the warfare that the Christians instigated.

Man is here on this earth, (based on the Ibrahimic religion) because of the punishment of one man: Adam. However, God is great and merciful, He gave the earth to mankind to use, take advantage of all the resources that are available, discover the secrets of the earth, and populate it. Most importantly, it is to be our resting place for an appointed term. If you look at the earth during the time of the Prophets and the earth today, one can see that man has made supreme advances. However, science, discoveries and inventions start with many failures. Many people lost their lives during the Industrial Revolution, the early trains polluted the air, and most of the industrial manufacturer's waste products seeped into the earth and polluted the ecological world. The early Christian inventors' learned from their mistakes but sometimes it cost lives, limbs, and the destruction of the earth. But in the long term discoveries, inventions and technologies are all well needed in the world today. In order to conduct his research, Mr. White used an automobile, typed his articles on a typewriter, watched TV, and he traveled by airplane or train. These are just three of some of the greatest inventions from man for man to use.

Today's white Christians are very aggressive in preserving their monopoly on the sciences, making discoveries and inventing new technologies. Everything was sought for the white Christian first. They know how to take natural resources from the earth of Africa and Asia; give pennies for the raw material, then sell the finished product in the west for hundreds of dollars, making the corporations millions of dollars and the investors on Wall Street happy. The white Christian race was one hundred percent guilty of abusing nature. Do you remember the American history of the Puritans and the Settlers that came from England to the New World? First, these Christian white people brought with them diseases, the pig, and weapons of mass destruction. The Christians' intentions were to enslave the Native American and when that did not work, they were happy that the native people died from the spread of disease. The wild pig or the boar ran across the country with its diseases, killing insects and other small animals that are now extinct. Even after converting the Native American people to Christianity, they were never accepted as brethren of the white Christians. Because they were treated as inferior beings, white Christians ethnically cleansed the Native Americans from the Atlantic Ocean to the Pacific Ocean.

The overfishing or hunting of whales in the 1800s and 1900s by American fishermen was a highly organized industry. The oil obtained from the whales' blubber was used for both lighting and lubricating purposes, and the bones of the whale were used to make a variety of useful household products. The overfishing and destruction of the seas from oil drilling were just some of the abuses that continue today.

The old clever United States government was enthusiastic and eager to use their atomic bomb during the Second World War in Europe. Some historians say that the US knew that the Japanese were flying warplanes in the air to attack Pearl Harbor and the US watched and let it happen. All of those innocent people sacrificed their lives for an unworthy government. Now that the US was a part of the war, they had the Atomic Bomb ready to deploy. However, it was said that Germany was still working on its version of the Atomic Bomb. Once all of the elements of warfare were presented, the vengeful and hotheaded American government did not hesitate to drop not one, but two Atomic bombs on Japan. The first bomb was a uranium gun-type device that had the code name, "Little Boy." It was dropped on the city of Hiroshima on August 6, 1945. The second bomb, a plutonium implosion-type device with the code name "Fat Man," was dropped on the city of Nagasaki three days later. These two cities experienced massive destruction and approximately 200,000 Japanese people (mostly civilians) died and suffered from acute injuries. The Americans set precedence by being the first to use nuclear weapons out of anger. Today, this was what we expect from "white Christian dominators." Although mankind had lived with war and violence throughout its history, the atomic bombings announced the arrival of a new and qualitatively different peril. This peril still threatens humanity: sudden, mass and indiscriminate destruction from a single weapon. From the vantage point of fifty years after these events, the atomic bombings and the end of World War II in the Pacific mark a turning point.[20]

Agent Orange was an herbicidal warfare program that the US military used during the Vietnam War from 1961 to 1971. As a result of spraying 20,000,000 US gallons of Agent Orange over Vietnamese agricultural land, 400,000 people were killed or maimed and 500,000 children were born with birth defects. In South Vietnam alone, an estimated 10 million hectares, 25 million acres, and 39,000 square miles of agricultural land were

---

[20] Internet: afa.org

ultimately destroyed. Furthermore, the people cannot drink the water or grow crops to feed themselves. People do not realize that white Christian domination influences the decisions that white racists make in order to destroy lives. These people were our elected officials (senators and representatives) all carrying out the orders of the evil white man in the White House.

White Christian powers were responsible for indiscriminate action against human life, the animal kingdom, plants and both living and non-living nature. They created chemical warfare, nuclear weapons, atomic warfare, and thermonuclear warfare; all major nuclear exchanges that have severe long term effects due to radiation release and the production of high levels of atmospheric pollution that have the potential to lead to a nuclear winter that could last for decades, centuries or even a millennium after the initial attack. They have created and used biological warfare with the use of biological toxins or infectious agents such as bacteria, viruses and fungi with the intent to kill or incapacitate humans, animals or plants as an act of war. Finally, these were just some of the chemical elements or compounds that the US government chose to reveal to the people. Because the US government was extremely evil, with a strong history of injustice and violence, there was a good probability that they have used chemical, nuclear, and biological warfare, along with sophisticated types of weaponry that the common man cannot comprehend.

First God freely gave man clean air, water and soil

but those resources required stewardship; and the dominating white man has failed at the task of being a steward. Their actions have caused disasters and catastrophes that some confuse as being "natural," but they were man-made problems. Nuclear energy was the cause of the number one man-made catastrophe. If the nuclear plant had an accident, radiation fills the air, water and soil. The end result was that the town becomes vacant because the people have to quickly leave. Many man-made catastrophes were caused by capital greed, and risky behavior in over drilling or digging for oil that causes leaks and kills wildlife contaminates water and threatens the fragile ecosystem.

Lastly over whaling continues in the world, using forest timber for heating, electricity generation or liquid biofuel could severely harm forests and accelerate global warming. The international organization to expose environmental abuse was called Greenpeace. They follow a Quaker denomination faith concept committed to nonviolence. Their objective was to stop global environmental abuse. Their first task was in 1971 to take nonviolent direct action against the United States' nuclear weapons testing. The perpetrators were governments, corporations and international bodies that duck, and dismiss issues of the problems, the responsibilities and the solutions. The over whaling continues, deforestation continues, the testing of nuclear weapons continues, and global warming is here to stay. Lastly because of capitalism greed for energy is out of control. All of the first world countries of Christian Europe and America have all the necessary energies, particularly heat. These countries do not share their energy technologies with the 3rd world country. Therefore don't blame the 3rd world countries for cutting down the forest to heat their homes in the winter month. Here again, the dominating white Christian world has an overwhelming abundance of energy and resource and the weak non-whites have zero.

World Politics

The United Nations was established to replace the flawed League of Nations in 1945 in order to maintain international peace and promote cooperation in solving international economic, social and humanitarian problems. The League of Nations failed because it could not stop the most violent European Christian countries from fighting each other. The United Nations should also be dismantled because the so-called world peace organizations still perpetuate conflict. The United Nations is first, pro-white Christian, second, pro-capitalism, and third pro-western; therefore, it is biased towards non-white people, non-Christian people and non-European countries. It is a particularly white Christian capitalistic racist organization. The United Nations is always late when it comes to helping the people in the continent of Africa and Asia. The United Nations is extremely reluctant to help the Arabs and Muslim people in their many conflicts. If your country practices a socialist economic system the United Nations does not recognize you. International law and international security allow the United Nations to put sanctions on countries in Africa and the Middle East but never on the USA, England and Israel. These dominating superpowers can break all the international laws, and international securities, start wars based on false intelligence, have surveillance on people all over the world, drop bombs on innocent people and the United Nations has a veil over their eyes and cotton in their ears because they do nothing to stop the violent aggressive white Christian secular countries.

Economic development and social progress... give me a break! Both of these agendas should be eradicated. The 2008 world economic crisis forced people to practice white Christian capitalism. This Christian capitalism cheats on people in the marketplace when buying a car, or a house. People are cheated in the finance world as well when investments and placing hope on Wall Street. Banks are the biggest crooks in the world today. They give the people less than 1% on their savings and charge over 29% on credit cards.

Social progress is another aim of the United Nations. The people of the world are in a social and moral decline. We live in a global world with the superpowers of the USA dictating behavior from the media, propaganda, Hollywood movies and TV shows. The USA's government promotes white Christian aggression and domination, the media tells lies, promotes capitalism, propagates homosexuality and the Hollywood industry promotes 100% violent TV shows and movies. Famine in Africa, overpopulation in Asia, wars in the Middle East, economic crises in Europe, and the AIDS epidemic continues to spread. What is the United Nations doing? Nothing! The distribution of food, medicine and supplies are all based on capitalism and if the USA can make a profit. If a country is poor then they likely have no clean water, food or the many basic necessities to survive.

The United Nations has issued a declaration on the rights of indigenous people to guide member-state national policies in protecting the collective rights of indigenous peoples to their culture, identity, language, employment, health, education and natural resources. The United Nations was organized by the white Christian dominating powers of mostly Europe and now the USA. These people look at the issues from the white dominating point of view. They write laws, and policies and change cultures based on the benefit of the conquering dominating white countries. Therefore, it does not benefit the natives and or indigenous people. The indigenous people are still at the mercy of their white dominating Christian conquers. The British Empire presently still has 13 colonies in the world, the United States Empire has two colonies, Samoa and Guam and the United Nations has made zero effort to decolonize or give freedom to these native people.

The United Nations should be a statistic company. They reported the ethnic cleansing of Rohingyas Muslim people living in the Arakan region. As of 2012, only 800,000 Rohingyas are living in Myanmar. The United Nations says that they are one of the most persecuted minorities in the world. As a result of systematic discrimination that they have endured in the past, many of them have migrated to Bangladesh and Malaysia and currently 300,000 Rohingya Muslims live in Bangladesh and 24,000 in Malaysia. The world is silent as Muslims are massacred in Myanmar. Because these people are not white Christians and do not live in Europe, there will be no help from the United Nations.

Before the 1992 genocide in Bosnia and Herzegovina, the Croatia Catholics, the Serbian Orthodox Christians and the Bosnian Muslims lived in harmony for over 500 years and for 40 years under communist rule. With the collapse of Communism in the 1990s and the launch of white Christian capitalism, Serbian Christian domination and ethnic cleansing of the mostly Muslim civilians occurred. The evil and cruel Christians always manage to have an effective organization, backed by a strong and disciplined military. They systematically went door to door capturing and putting men and women in concentration camps where they were gang-raped, tortured, starved and murdered. In 1993, the United Nations watched and very little media coverage exposed what was going on. Bill Clinton, the President, was too busy having improper sexual affairs with Monica Lewinsky, which led to his impeachment. After over 100,000 Muslims lost their lives, the United Nations told the Bosnian Muslims to give up their weapons because they would have protection from UN peacekeepers in the enclaves' safe areas. In 1995, the Christian Orthodox Serbian committed the largest massacre in European history since World War II, while the so-called UN peacekeepers watched and took statistical information, and not a single shot was fired by the UN.

In 1994, the Rwandan Genocide mass murdered an estimated amount of 800,000 people in East Africa. The majority, the Hutu people were against the 20% minority Tutsi, who had controlled power since the colonization days of Germany and Belgium. The former secretary of the United Nations, Boutros Boutros-Ghali, and an Egyptian Christian supplied weapons to the Hutu which led to up to a million deaths. Here again, is the perfect example of why the UN should be forced to dismantle. This so-call-peace organization gave the Hutu weapons to continue the war which only caused more atrocities and genocide. It would have been wise for the UN to have started a truce. But because they are an organization of white Christians, they promote these two words: hatred and violence.

In 1935 Italian soldiers commanded by Marshal invaded Ethiopia. The war lasted seven months before an Italian victory was declared. The invasion was condemned by the League of Nations, though not much was done to end the hostility. In 1935, Italy used mustard gas during the invasion of Ethiopia on civilian villages. By doing this, the Geneva Protocol was ignored, which was signed seven years earlier. The Italian military dropped mustard gas in bombs, sprayed it from airplanes, and spread it in powdered form on the ground. 150,000 chemical casualties were reported, mostly from mustard gas. In the aftermath of the war, Italy annexed Ethiopia, uniting it with Italy's other colonies in eastern Africa to form the new colony of Italian East Africa, and adopted the title Emperor of Abyssinia. Hailie Selassie, the Emperor of Ethiopia, opposed the Italian invasion. He appealed to the League of Nations and the League of Nations declared Italy the aggressor. In Washington, FDR invoked an act in the Ethiopian conflict but followed a middle course. The end result was a big zero from these white Christian rulers and their so-called international organization. The rulers of Africa and the non-white people of the world need to reflect on history. History will tell them that these white bodies do not represent them in the least; the US government was more concerned about getting more underpriced oil from the ignorant Saudis as opposed to the preservation of humanity. However, Italy withdrew after five years of occupation.

Some people just blow with the direction of the wind, the Holy Roman Empire became the country of Germany these Roman Catholic people became Nazis with a totalitarian state ruled by Adolf Hitler, which led to slave labor across Europe, Jews, political prisoners, criminals, homosexuals, gypsies. The mentally ill were all imprisoned in concentration camps then mass genocide of the Jews between 1939 and 1942. There was nothing holy about, "The Holy Roman Empire" with their aggressive atrocity on weaker nations. But after becoming Nazism the German people became their true selves. At the end of the day, Nazi Germany and the Aryan people were Christians.

Christianity and the bible do not cure evil. Like the Klan who is also Protestant Christian terrorists, extremists and murderers. The Christian Bible and the church did not stop their evil agendas.

Some recent massacres that the United Nations has only taken statistical notes.

Country	Year	Kill
Cambodia genocide	1975-1979	1.4m
Khojaly massacre (Azerbaijani) people	1992	613
Vukovar massacre by Serbs people	1991	264
Ethnic cleansing of Georgians	1992-1993	17,000-22,000

Ibrahim Mosque Massacre in the West Bank 1994, 29 killed and 150 wounded by a Jew, Baruch Goldstein

Srebrenica massacre of Bosnians 1995   8,000 people

Qana massacre on Lebanese Muslims 1996 by Israeli   106 people

Andijan massacre in Uzbekistan 2005   1500 Muslim protestors

A democracy is a form of government where the people elect officials and representatives. The constitution provides the basis of governmental authority, limits government power by mandating free elections, and guarantees free speech. Political institutions allow gradual change to ensure economic and political stability. Rapid and destabilizing change is curbed by a system of checks and balances that distributes power among the three branches of government legislative, executive and judicial, among the federal, state and local governments. Sounds good on paper, huh?

The aggressive white Christians have created a lopsided world through their domination, capitalism and unmerciful military powers. The USA and Europe have the resources and technological prowess needed to sustain life. They have taken natural resources from Africa to better their lives and in return, they have given back pennies per pound. Before the European colonization of thousands of African people, they were enslaved by other Africans and Arabs. During the colonial life under white Christian humiliation, discrimination, and injustice were rampant. Even today people continue to lose their lives due to the seeds of unhappiness planted by the white conquerors. Following colonization, Africans had to fight for their freedom. Many lost lives from the superior weaponry of the extremist white European Christians. Furthermore, in the white Christian finale, they decimated small villages, destroyed agriculture and raped Africa's land, depleting all-natural resources. Africa remains the third world because of the aftermath of the colonial power that put puppet rules into practice, where greed-based Christian capitalism ruled, making it impossible to achieve social progress. There are still impoverished countries in Africa. The Africans had a difficult time getting their natural resources to the global marketplace to make a good profit for the whole continent and Africa continues to experience poor leadership.

The continent of Africa did not benefit from the agricultural revolution, the industrial medical revolution and today's information-globalization revolution. Because Europeans and white Christian people discover things first, they do not share in their technologies and if the country is poor they will not be able to afford advancement anyways. Malaria, for example, does not exist in Europe or the USA, but they have the vaccine for their people. However, the place where it is needed, sub-Saharan Africa, only has small quantities for their large population. The Christian countries have an overwhelming abundance of food, water, medicine, clothing, appliances, etc., and do not run out of supplies and or resources, whereas Africa is just the opposite. The corrupt leaders of Africa are the most problematic source of controversy for the continent. The dominating powers of the white Christian league (the USA, the Europeans and the United Nations) quickly put sanctions on these small, poor African countries. The end result is civilian hardship while the corrupted leader lives off the fat of the land. When listening to the media, the US government is depicted as being pro-white Christian capitalists. The greedy rich people have to increase their wealth before trickle-down economics takes effect and the needy receive aid. Furthermore, the media targets poor people and the Islamic faith as the source of blame for all the problems in the world today.

During the 2011 republican presidential race for

the president, a Republican candidate stated, "The Muslims in America were forcing the Christians to practice the Sharia." This was such a nebulous statement. Although he knows that the Sharia means Islamic law, he should give examples, and tell the people what particular laws were forced on the Christian. Other than that he is lying and wants to create conflicts. The Muslims in America dare not tell any fast-food chain to cook their hamburgers on a separate cooking grill from the bacon (pork grill). Therefore all Muslims that eat fast food most likely are eating pork. After a college or business meeting, the members always order pepperoni and sausages pizza never vegetarian pizza, therefore, the Christians proudly tell the hungry Muslims to just take the pepperoni and sausages off. Such disgusting circumstances Muslims are a force to comply within this society. But who is dominated? Who has to submit to who's ethical and social laws? Every loft of bread, ice cream and bakery product in the stores across the country has the ingredient mono-diglycerides which are 100% lard, so the people are eating pork. There are so many more situations and scenarios that Muslims have to accept in this Christian/secular society. Furthermore, the Muslims dare not open their mouths to complain and challenge the dominating western civilization lifestyle. Therefore this candidate is practicing his Politian skills of lying to the people.

Lastly, historian says the first generations of Muslims were the best generation. Know that the first generation was all converts coming out of paganism, polytheism, Jews and Christians. Particularly the Christians when they accept Islam, they immediately want to wage war on their own Christian/secular governments. Perhaps they know and see the corruption of their government and they see the violent nature of their government towards the Islamic world. But the Quran says new Muslims have little to no faith. Therefore a Sheikh said to a young man, who wanted to go into battle, "say there is no god but God and Muhammad is the last messenger of God," then make your five prays a day and make them on time. Fast the month of Ramadan and read and study the Quran, give a small percent of your wealth to the poor and make Hajj if you can afford it. If you can complete these tasks then you now have some faith. Now you are ready for a big challenge (jihad). Within this time period if you have seen a young beautiful girl wearing hijab and Islamic clothing then ask her father for her hand in marriage. If he says yes, get marriage, love her, satisfy her and in nine months baby come; now you have a family. This is grace, this is beauty, and this may be a better jihad, young man. And this is Islam!

The Guantanamo Bay US naval base and detention camp in Cuba holds persons alleged to be unlawful combatants captured in Afghanistan and Iraq. At least that is what the US government claims. This place is a perfect example of white Christian domination. The UN or the Geneva Convention has no say in what goes on there, their eyes are closed and cotton is in their ears. The prisoners, mostly Muslim men, have no rights or no international protection. They suffered abuse and torture by the Bush Administration and they have not been accused or charged with a crime. In a state of limbo, they have endured waterboarding, a method of torture and other sophisticated methods of torture that will make any man break down and say what the enemy wants. The intelligent and practicing Muslims have every right to protect themselves from white Christian aggression. These two wars are based on white Christian arrogance, domination, the use of their weapons of mass destruction and hatred of the Muslim people. If the US government did not represent the white, mostly Protestant civilians, they would surely rise up and produce hundreds of militias to fight foreign invasion as well as the US government force.

In conclusion, there has been no world peace since the United Nations came into existence. Therefore, the United Nations has completely failed in all its aims, objectives and goals. The United Nations is a pro-white, Christian, racist organization. The organization promotes pro-capitalism for the world economy, extremely violent actions and an unjust organization. The United Nations supports the destruction of the Islamic faith and the ethnic cleansing of Muslims all over the world. The United Nations supports white Christian capitalism when it cheats the people, overcharges for gasoline, gives consumers high interest on credit cards, and problematizes the terms of loans when buying a car and a house. The United Nations has absolutely no power over the new global powers the United States Empire, the British Empire and Israel. These countries can start a war with their weapons of mass destruction and begin to murder and slaughter hundreds of thousands of innocent civilians while the UN sits back and takes notes. There are many problems in this world we live in and with the aggressive nature of white capitalistic and murderous Christians; things are not going to get better. The United Nations is a disgrace to the humanity of the world. The sad fact of the matter is that so many persecuted ethnic groups wish, hope and pray that the United Nations will come to their rescue, but unfortunately, the UN only helps white Christians first, Jews second and countries with liquidity in natural resources.

For the United Nations to be effective, it should attack the conflict head-on. The UN should go directly to the country with their diplomats and the military force, talk with both parties, create a truce, and then do what is necessary to end the problem. They should not take sides based on Christianity, capitalism and race. The United Nations continues to fail in the category of world peace because they are unable to provide the security of nations from neighboring threats, they do not uphold the principles of justice and international law, and they continuously fail at settling international disputes and the principle of equal rights and self-determination of peoples is unclear to them as a whole. Their focus and concern should be to solve international problems of economic, social, and cultural degradation that dangerously impede the humanity of mankind. They have proven that they have the capacity to always fail when promoting and encouraging respect for human rights and for fundamental freedoms for all without distinctions being made as to race, sex, language, or religion. The UN should be a center for harmonizing the actions of nations in the attainment of these common goals. They have failed in all four statements of the purposes of the United Nations (Article 1). Let's ask the Muslim people in Burma (Myanmar), the Middle East, Africa, the Aborigines, the non-whites of New Zealand and the Native Americans if they have respectable human rights.

If the government is practicing evil deeds and individuals are a member of the government should the individuals stop the behavior or indulge in the practice too? If you are a government soldier and the command was to slaughter unarmed innocent people should you do this? Believe it or not, there are some morally correct white Christian soldiers in the US military. Bradley Manning a PFC in rank has a good soul, a conscious, and chose not to murder innocent civilians. First, the PFC ranking is third from the bottom, secondly, these soldiers mostly take orders only and thirdly, most of the top-secret stay at the top with the Lieutenants, Captains and Majors and or higher up the Colonels and Generals. It is so sad there is no international organization to stop the United States government from destroying peace, crimes against humanity, and war crimes. They force their low-ranking soldiers to do the dirty work of being overly aggressive in their tactics of slaughter and massacre of mankind.

Everything in the world revolves around pro-white Christian domination. The people either submit to their evil behaviors or die from their sophisticated weaponry. This superpower has violated all of the UN's purposes. This white Christian country loves instigating and entering wars, from the Vietnam War in the sixties to the criminal attacks made on Muslim countries today. The US government has slaughtered, massacred, murdered, and killed well over 50 million innocent men, women, babies, embryos, etc... In addition, they have destroyed nature, air, water, soil, ecology, plants and animal life. They spread diseases all over the world and the US government, the media and the entertainment industry blame poor people and the Islamic faith for the problems in the world. Finally, when they make a movie that historically interprets the many atrocities, America is a party too; once again blame is placed on non-white people and non-Christians. There is always a lie at the end of the movie that makes the Americans the protagonist or hero. What a powerful and clever devil he is!

Chapter XV

When Will It End

Who should rule the world? Are the people who rule compassionate, impartial, or sympathetic? The United States government, a proven racist, rules the world as racist white Christians, overflowing with hatred, violence and secularism. The 100 white senators are like high school bullies who use aggressive tactics and behavior to start wars based on false intelligence. They attack countries that have no standing army, navy, air force or marines. They seize upon the opportunity to menace the poor, uneducated and defenseless. The most damaging effect that white Christians have on any race of non-white people or non-Christian people was colonization or the process of complete conquest through military force. As we learned, when this happens, the peoples' culture (religion, language, education, heritage, lifestyle) was forever destroyed. The USA instigates wars because they have weapons of mass destruction and their opponents do not. Because Americans act under the guise of Christianity, they have an excuse to propagate hate toward people who are of a different faith, race, political agenda and economic system. This was completely erroneous and needs to stop! The USA is making weapons of mass destruction and sophisticated surveillance equipment 24 hours a day. Their dedication to arms demonstrates that they need to start wars to practice using their weaponry, craft and technologies. The USA and UK persecute mankind, predominantly non-Christian people all over the globe. May God allows these antichrist people to perish (the 100 white senators, the 435 representatives and the man that lives at 1600 Pennsylvania Avenue)!

When you watch the news, you can see that the white Christian soldiers are slaughtering and massacring people in Iraq and Afghanistan. The USA military does not fight a uniform army in these countries. American forces murder innocent men, women, children, infants, and embryos; not to mention destroy property, houses, villages, livestock and crops. The news has shown how white Christian soldiers dominated the Iraqi people by attacking them with dogs, sodomizing male prisoners, posing for photos of themselves standing over dead corpses, and urinating on dead corpses. As if all of the above does not suffice, they enjoy watching the Quran burn. These white soldiers believe and know they are dominant. Mobilized with hatred and violence, they say and write evil and suffer no repercussions for their evil thoughts and actions. All of the military people that are charged with a crime may serve one month in prison or administrative leave with pay. This was not justice and the Arab and Muslim people need to understand that they will never attain justice in a white Christian courtroom. An old saying, "sticks and stones may break my bones but words can never hurt me." Although the beginning of the phrase is true, the second part is false because the words are powerful and words hurt. The media glorifies the soldiers with honor and valor. The more tours and murders that were committed, the higher the soldier will grow in rank and pay. The US government does not want the media to show the evils of the war because the public will see that American soldiers break all the ethics of the war. "From the Halls of Montezuma to the shores of Tripoli we will fight our country's battles," says the Marine Song. Meaning American soldiers and marines take no prisoners. From World War I, World War II, the Vietnam War, the Gulf Wars and now the Islamic wars that are taking place in Iraq and Afghanistan, American policies have always been: take no prisoners. So what happens when the enemy surrenders? Well, the Christian soldiers never run out of ammunition and they were always equipped with an overflow of adrenaline. Hateful blood journeys through their veins and they follow orders to murder mankind.

Who should rule the world? Can a man from North Africa rule, from a sub-Saharan rule or maybe South Africa? All of these regions and people have been completely conquered by white Christian militaries and their governments. They have been thought acculturated, Christianized, westernized, beaten, and enslaved. They do not have it in their soul to dominate world politics, commerce and wars. They can only control their small ethnic tribes and many times these rulers become tyrants. The colonization of Africa destroyed the souls of all of Africa from Tunisia to South Africa to Senegal to Somalia. Can the Arab Muslim people in the Middle East rule the world again? There are too many religious and tribal conflicts that present problems for ruling the world as they did before. They are at a disadvantage because they do not have superior weapons, but they do have tyrants and puppets as leaders, political issues, weak economies and the loss of control over Palestine. Maybe the Chinese, Japanese or Southeast Asian people can rule the world. These people originally were nice, polite, non-aggressive, and non-dominating. They do not have it in their soul to dominate, conquer, or start wars that kill large populations. When looking at the arrogant white man, the West has taught generation after generation to be arrogant, aggressive, and dominant. From a young age, they have no fear of God and they believe that they are better than the rest of the world. Indoctrinated as children, they believe in the insane principles of White Christian Domination and supremacy they take it to another level as adults. Therefore, world Christian domination will continue. If the method of hatred and violence works, why change it?

Should the people of the USA and UK be happy and proud that they can kill and murder Muslims all over the world at random? They must because they do so when they see fit, without any liability or just cause. Should they be happy that they destroy two ancient civilizations, Iraq and now Syria? Should white dominating Christians be proud that they have vehicles that destroy such as many different types of helicopters, F1, F12, stealth bombers, warplanes, battleships and now surveillance devices and unman drones? There are missiles in the Mediterranean Sea, Arabian Sea, and the Indian Ocean ready to aim and fire at innocent Arabs and Muslim families. The soldiers and advertisements say that they are fighting for freedom. The Iraq War is based on hatred towards Saddam Hussein, knowingly false intelligence and pure arrogance. The 99 white racist senators knew that Iraq did not have weapons of mass destruction or nuclear weapons. The United Nations had a team of about 700 inspectors who inspected the whole country numerous times with the Hans Blip of Sweden as the Chief Weapons Inspector. Hans Blip called George Bush and Tony Blair madmen with the same mind frame as the witch hunter of the "medieval Roman Catholic Church." The Bush administration, Dick Cheney, Collin Powell and Donald Rumsfeld all knew they could start a war in the Middle East and easily defeat this Arab country. They knew that they could easily start a war in Afghanistan and defeat the Taliban. The people of Iraq and their government had absolutely nothing to do with 911; the same with Afghanistan people and the Taliban had nothing to do with 911. Also, Iraq and Afghanistan were not a threat to Israel and or New York City. They do not have missiles that can reach Tel Aviv or New York City; they do not have a working air force, navies and battleships either. The media in the USA (NBC, ABC, CBS, FOX, CNN, NPR, etc...) all tell the American people lies and disseminate distorted information.

Within the last twenty years, the United States Empire and the British Empire have abused their United Nations resolution preferences by starting these two wars. Who is Prince Harry firing at from a helicopter? How many innocent Afghan citizens has he murdered? Why is England in this war in the first place? Due to his family's history of murdering people around the clock, Prince Harry was carrying out the historical mission of the British monarchy by murdering scores of people. Surely he qualifies to be the next King.

The Arab Muslim people have let their guard down. As long as they follow Western Civilization and their secular system the Arab Muslim people will continue to be third world people and second class citizens in their own country. All of the Arab rulers hate the Islamic faith and this disdainfully was seen in the gradual dilution of the Islamic faith that had occurred over the years. The Arab leaders want their people to be secular and follow a sinful, western-influenced lifestyle. If a third-world country is a puppet to the US government, then it is also a puppet to Israel and this is absolutely why the Muslims cannot defend themselves. Israel alone can destroy, conquer and take more land from any Muslim country. If all of the Muslim countries together attack Israel, Israel will still manage to defeat every last one of them. Why? Because the Muslim governments do not represent Islam, they do not represent their people, their military is weak, they have no modern technologies, their economy is broken and the whole of the Islamic world is divided and they all hate their neighbors. The Arab countries need to understand that the US government is not their friend or ally. White evangelist Christians and this secular government hate Islam and have intentions to depopulate Jerusalem of its Muslim population and destroy the Dome of the Rock. Egypt, Saudi Arabia, Jordan and now Iraq and Afghanistan are all puppets. All of these countries obey the US government and in return, these governments do not help or support their people, but support the USA instead; by virtue, supporting Israel.

And lastly, the Arabs, Islam and Muslim issues first, the Egyptian situation the people need to give the new government time, second, the Syrian situation because the Assad government is rule based on a Shia tribe called the Alawites, who help the British during the early 20th-century occupation, they are presently supported by the USA, UK and Israel and the rebels are Sunni Muslims that the USA, UK and Israel hate therefore this problem is far from resolved. And thirdly the Arab people need to get some binoculars, to see that the western/secular/Christian world doesn't like them as a people, they need to pull up their pants and stop allowing the west to dominate them, their best criterion, and ammunition is the Quran and the tradition of the Prophet because surely the west is not on their side when it comes to policy, economy and the military. The country of Iran is just a big pussy-cat with no political clout and the US knows this so they play the political game of sanctions. These two Muslim countries Pakistan and Saudi Arabia should not allow the white Christian forces of the USA and UK to have an air force and military bases on their grounds to murder Muslim citizens using drone attacks. This is purely against the Islamic faith. Particularly the Wahhabists and the Salafists of Saudi Arabia know the law and what the Prophet said about having an infidel the (USA and UK) occupying the Muslim lands. These two countries represent the values of the USA and UK there they represent Israel and furthermore and most important they do not represent their own people.

The similarity between the white race, white corporations, and white governments are like the Star Trek TV show and the movie Avatar. First, the overly aggressive, Captain Kirk, attacks, fires the first shot, falls in love with a green alien girl and pursues the objective of getting rich by seeking or taking precious metals (gold) or natural resources. Space as a physical setting for the plot does not matter. The same plot lines can be translated into stories that take place on an island or a continent. The fleet onboard the spaceship seeking the final frontier is much like the European explorers who sailed across the Atlantic. Both parties, fictional and nonfictional, used an arsenal of weapons of mass destruction, and never asked the natives to trade or bargain, or to be business partners. Ask the indigenous group featured in the Avatar movie if the white soldiers and staff sought commerce or knowledge about their civilization before attacking, killing and slaughtering the native people. At the end of every conquest tale, the white corporation becomes rich from stolen resources, the white government receives all of the glory and the white race expands. The expansion causes more trouble, hatred, violence and the continuance of madness.

"Space/earth . . . the final frontier; these are the voyages of the United States Empire." Although the USA is young, they are the most aggressive and arrogant country.

They have proven this by their will to dominate murder, kill, slaughter, massacre, torture, and sodomize the New Worlds. They are successfully making mankind capitalist, individualist, violent criminals, and polytheists and in doing so they destroy civilizations, the environment and the ecosystem. This government has made a promise to continue to boldly go and put sanctions on the weak and the oppressed, to pollute everything in its path, from the land to outer-space, and the air and water in between. Wildlife and nature were abused in the process and people are brainwashed into believing that voting and their man-made three-god religion will guarantee the fixing."

Jimmy Carter Accuses the US of 'Widespread Abuse of Human Rights'
By Amy Bingham, ABC News
A former U.S. president is accusing the current president of sanctioning the "widespread abuse of human rights" by authorizing drone strikes to kill suspected terrorists. Jimmy Carter, America's 39 the president, denounced the Obama administration for "clearly violating" 10 of the 30 articles of the Universal Declaration of Human Rights, writing in a New York Times op-ed on Monday that the "United States is abandoning its role as the global champion of human rights." "Instead of making the world safer, America's violation of international human rights abets our enemies and alienates our friends," Carter wrote. While the total number of attacks from unmanned aircraft, or drones, and the resulting casualties are murky, the New America Foundation estimates that in Pakistan alone 265 drone

strikes have been executed since January 2009. [21]

"How are you," "I beg your pardon," "good morning," "she's a cutie," "have a nice day," "pleased to meet you!" So polite, generous, courteous, charitable and jolly are the white Christian people today. The question is how did they change from their history of malevolence that spans over two millenniums? Can credit be given to the Church? Perhaps it was legislation, Hollywood or the media. It is possible that any one of these entities persuaded, instilled and transferred the evil vices and behaviors of whites to the Black race. Surely there are many unhappy and mean blacks in the USA and Africa because of poverty and the lack of education. On the other hand, the white race is educated, organized, and they are professionals at skillfully planning long-term attacks on those they deem as subordinates under their leadership. Remember, although times have changed, cleverness and arrogance were embedded in the white man's chromosome, DNA and soul.

Finally, the white race mascot should be the carnivorous dog-like species, "the Hyena," because these creatures are malicious, treacherous, arrogant, boastful, reviler and irreconcilable. Carl T. Roland wrote in his book about the race wars that will come. This point of the veil was strictly local and he did not see the big picture. The white race of Europe has completely subdued black Africa 300 hundred years ago. They have subdued the smaller built yellow man of Southeast Asia and also the people of

---

[21] Internet: yahoo news

India. The redman's defeat was an easy victory for white Americans. And the black Americans within the country are but brainwash submissive followers only and they don't see the bigger picture. Next, are the economic wars and issues of the aggressive white capitalist attacking a different economic system? The USA and British went beyond saying we don't like the communist economic system but they make policies to destroy it. The white race of France and the USA may have lost the Vietnam War against the smaller yellow man but after 1989 the USSR now Russia has become capitalist. The only good result of the ending of communism was the freeing of the many Eastern European countries. Lastly, the attack on religion by these white gentiles' people, before there was an Americas, the white race put the many sects of Christianity in checkmate. With the ferocious attack of white secular Christian on the Muslim civilization in the middle, the Muslims won the ending wars using the sword. But today the unmerciful white race has a superior weapon therefore the Muslims have to submit or be ethnic clean. The fact, that all the Sunni Muslim rulers (kings and presidents) kissed the left hand of Christian rulers while the Christian spits on the neck of these Arab rulers which is the ultimate disgrace.

Chapter XVI

And the Madness Continues

Should Christians follow a covenant
that gives limitations or should they
follow the white founding fathers
"Bill of Rights" Constitution that gives
unlimited transgression freedoms?

Although the countries under Western Civilization are all mostly secular, the civilians and the acting government people are all Christians. All 100 white USA senators, for example, are all some kind of Protestant Christian, 434 Christians are representatives with one representative who is the first Sunni Muslim, Keith Ellison. Western Civilization and its secular system can be very subtle and hypocritical. These secular systems are full of violence in society. The people have no religion, no fear of God, but chips are on their shoulders and revenge lives in their hearts. Every day people are being murdered senselessly throughout the country in every city-state. The Massacre in Connecticut Friday 14, 2012, a 24-year-old boy who was upset with his mother shot her then went to an elementary school and shot 20 children and 6 staff members. This US constitutional secularism system will never stop promoting the sin of violence, sex, drugs and many other criminal behaviors because the justice system and the government profits from criminal obscenities. People need to find spiritual truth and put it into practice, but this is difficult when people are told to chase capitalism and materialism by any means necessary.

The saying, "You are what you eat," should be

translated into, "you do what you hear and see," as well. In the Middle East or in Arab-speaking countries, the Quran is in the air. People hear the recital of the Quran in the marketplace, in taxi cabs and at the mosques. The Quran is constantly admonishing the Arab-speaking people telling them to be righteous, seek the path to heaven and obey God and the Prophet. Let's go to the USA, in this country in the marketplace people will hear a variety of music in the malls, the athletic clubs, cars, department stores and even at coffee cafés where people like to write. Music triggers memories, some music encourages the making of love and sex, and some music is political, but the worse music is the relatively new innovation of "Rap Music." Listeners are told to degrade girls and the lyrics propagate violence. Surely all Americans have a flat-screen TV in their home to watch all of their favorite violent TV shows, movies, and news programs that is broadcasted 24 hours a day. The theme of this paragraph, "You are What You Eat," leads to the notion that people also, "Do What They Hear and See." The United States of America is the most violent country in the history of the world. Between New York City, Chicago, Los Angeles and Atlantic City, well over 100 people lose their lives every week. The church is closed Monday through Saturday and there is no religious covenant coming from any of the many Christian churches; therefore there is no discipline, morals, ethics, obedience to religion and or God in everyday life. There are many Americans that strictly obey and learn from the radio, white Christian Hollywood writers of TV shows and movies. Americans listening to the 6 o'clock news will always hear about senseless murders, soldiers raping girls, bank robberies and many other criminal acts daily. Believe it or not, the constitution, the 100 white pro-Christian Senators and the Republican Party actually want people to kill and murder each other. The core of socialization in the USA is capitalism (spend more money) and criminal acts the courts make lots of money and keep the church and or religion in the closet. Understand that white Christian people enjoy being controlled by pro-white aggressive Christian legislators, and then Hollywood makes a movie about the situation and the people are further brainwashed.

Men are so simple and ready to obey the one who deceives. Deceptive people will always find people who are willing to be deceived. "The end justifies the means" is interpreted by some to mean that whatsoever is required to get the desired results will be done, regardless of the methods used. It doesn't matter whether these methods are legal or illegal, fair or foul, kind or cruel, the truth or lies, democratic or dictatorial, good or evil. White Christians make bombs fall from the sky and merciless soldiers from England and the USA aggressively attack innocent civilians and destroy two predominantly Muslim countries. But there is a God in heaven full of justice, so He punishes the white Christian perpetrator with hurricanes, tornadoes, earthquakes, flooding, landslides, and wildfires. Environmental damage, human loss and financial loss are forms of punishment that man cannot control. But who can be seen grieving at the end of the day? The most powerful dominating Christian was the British Empire, next to the Holy Roman Empire but today the United States Empire is right at the top with a blood-stained history. Despite the exploitation of Native Americans and Africans, the white race still has a preference, status, political power, economic power, media influence and worst of all, secular power.

Democracy is a form of government for the people, corporations and rich people, it allows the citizens to participate directly or through political representatives, the creation of laws, and some social-economic, and cultural conditions that enable the free and equal practice of political self-determination.

Therefore in the USA, one ethnic group can form an organization based on any agenda (for the good of the people or the destruction of the people) and if the people's agenda has political representatives, the organization will most likely be successful. The perfect example of this is the Ku Klux Klan. Although many of its members committed murder and engaged in other heinous acts, because we live in a democracy, these men were still elected to represent the racist people of America. The white race has preference/status; they have moved up in the government and have become senators and presidents. Again in a democracy, if a privileged group wants to control and eliminate the dark race they can do so with support from all three levels of the government.

They will accomplish their objective even though it's immoral.

White Protestant Christian people know how to take advantage of a democratic government and Black Christian people do not. The National Rifle Association is America's number one foremost defender of the Second Amendment, "the right of the people to keep and bear arms." Baseball, apple pie and violence are symbols of the American creed and so are guns. Weapons have always been a necessity, whether guns were used to hunt four-legged animals or to kill two-legged people. Although we never had a major war within the borders of the USA, a war exists within our minds and souls. The people want assault weapons and the white Protestant Christian race always gets what they want. The NRA is a very powerful organization, with lots of money, plenty of members and most importantly, the political support (representatives, senators and even Presidents) needed to have a successful agenda. In a democratic society, we love violence and the government will stand behind the people even though violence destroys lives. Hundreds of senseless inner-city murders by the black race are committed every day but this benefits the privileged race, the white Protestant Christians. The black Protestant Christians will not dare to go to their local representatives or state senators and ask for measures to stop inner-city violence. Inner-city problems are seen as black Christian people's problems, not the democracy (the American peoples') problem. Over the years, hundreds of thousands of black people have lost their lives from gun violence and this has actually been supported by the US government, the NRA and the media. Now, rich upper-class white Protestant Christian boys have access to their parents' destructive weapons and they plot massacres, killing people of all ages. But, because this is a white crime against white people, the government intervenes and writes another worthless legislation.

In this democratic society if your agenda goes against the King James white Protestant Christian Bible but the people have support from local, state and federal governments. Eventually, these agendas will manifest themselves in society even though it is an evil and against the scriptures. Homosexuality and same-sex marriage, are a true abomination, a major sin, the destruction of the human race and a painful agony disease that will kill the people. In this white Christian society, there is an extremely powerful organization called the media and or the Hollywood entertainment industry. These people promote evil 24 hours a day, they dramatize the sin, making it enjoyable then subconsciously implanted it in the minds of the youth to accept and experiment with this destructive behavior. In 2008 the first black Protestant Christian President was against this sexual behavior, but in 2012 during his presidential campaigning President Obama visited the Los Angeles area two times and pandered to the gay community who contributed enormous amounts of money. Therefore, he was forced to change his views on gay marriage and sexual issues. We live in a secular white Protestant dominating Christian fornicating and violent society. Between the ages of 15 and 31, young people start practicing their free love rights. The boyfriend-girlfriend syndrome fall in love, break up, jealousy, grief, rebounding (jumping from one relationship to another) and lastly catches one of many sexually transmitted diseases, and all these attributes are the same in the gay community. The whole gay community is a sex base agenda; a sodomy agenda for the US government to ratify their behavior is to tell the whole world community to be ready to catch HIV and then AIDS. The end result hundreds of angry infected gay guys will share and spread this deadly disease to innocent young girls and boys; and this again is now supported by senators, the man in the white house and many democratic people of the USA.

The most powerful institution in the history of mankind is the media and the Hollywood entertainment industry. Together, they teach, influence, persuade, tell stories, tell lies, and confuse the truth. The protagonist and antagonist are thematic elements of every TV show, movie, sitcom, talk show and even documentary. The goal of each median is to blame the good guy and to make the evil villain the hero. The people that run the industry are all millionaires, have political clout, and have individual agendas that they force the democracy (the people) to recognize and accept. Looking at the Hollywood industry starting with silent movies, you see the white race in action with all of their clout and status. The criminal nature of early American gangsters, the dishonest and untrustworthy businessmen and the drunken westerner killing everything in sight is a part of the American ego. The white Christian Hollywood industry is aware of the power they have to control the minds of the people with support from the news media writers. They also have tremendous control over people's thoughts and behaviors. The US government dare not tell the Hollywood industry to stop making crime-based TV shows and multi-action violent movies. The same with sex-based TV shows, movies and talk shows. Nobody blames white Protestant Christian Hollywood, but they do blame the black Christian peoples' rap music industry. The church is closed and the institution of the church has no voice. Because sin is a practice, they do not see their sinful ways. If the people continue to allow a filthy secular government system to rule over them, then we the people will perish. As a secular society filled with people who lack faith, people place their faith in the glitz and glamour of Hollywood.

On a daily basis, families across the country watch the evening world news with conviction and the white newsman looks the people straight in the eye and lies to them. All of the reported news in the USA is pro-white Protestant Christian, pro-capitalism, pro-secular, and pro-Zionism. With that said, the camera only shows the people a very narrow view of information. If the people of America travel and see the world, when they return home and watch the evening news, they will see and hear the lies. The news today is saying that American soldiers are fighting for American freedom and the American people foolishly believe this. What have the people of Afghanistan done? Please name one aggressive action the people of Afghanistan did against the people of New York City, London or Tel Aviv? Second, the USA media said, after 911 that Al Qaeda which consists of mostly Saudi Arabia Muslims and a couple of North African but no Afghanistan Muslims or Taliban Muslims.

In 2001, if the American people could comprehend the intelligence of the secret service and their incredible surveillance devices, they would have been able to conclude that dropping bombs was not necessary. All of the USA's three secret services, the CIA, the FBI, and the NSA could easily enter Afghanistan and locate the Al-Qaeda members and murder them all. However, the USA and the United Kingdom are bullies. Both parties knew they could win a war against this weak country, so they practiced using their new weaponry by bombing innocent Muslim people and destroying infrastructure and villages. They made it their mission to make life miserable for these people. The end result is that American "freedom fighters" have murdered, killed, slaughtered and massacred over a hundred thousand Afghanistan citizens that had absolutely nothing to do with Al- Qaeda, 911 and or the Taliban. This war is now over 10 years old, the international security assistance force continues to force the USA and UK's political, economic and social systems on these people. What happened to freedom? Freedom must be defined as nothing but the practice of the white dominating Christian way of life. White Christian domination continues to spread and conquer the Islamic world, destroying country after country. The media continues to give false information about this war nevertheless, white Protestant Christians the so-called freedom fighters depopulating the Muslim world.

The white Christian powers have done an excellent job in the past using vaccinations to eradicate the many early chronic diseases that they intentionally spread to all of the world population. However, one white man is given credit for the spreading of a relatively new chronic disease or virus called AIDS and HIV. One can draw conjectures as to how this happened. Maybe he was in the jungles of Africa and raped a chimpanzee or a gorilla, then being that he was a promiscuous homosexual, flew to New York and then to California knowingly probably something was wrong but continue to have sex with as many male partners as possible. The virus then spread because any homosexual male can easily have sex with girls, women and prostitutes; and by the 1990's it is an epidemic, with cases in all the states, England and Europe, Africa and Asia with no cure in sight. The power of the white men, when syphilis pop-up in the 1920s the US government said, for a couple to get married they must take a syphilis test. However, in the mid-1990 with AIDS/ HIV epidemic at its peak, the US government said no need to take any communicable diseases test to get married. "And you call this a government for the people." Why not? Because this chronic epidemic started out as a white homosexual disease! The black race was always open to obtaining the white man's evil burdens, within the next two decades millions of non-white people all over the world lost their lives to this disease. Today the homosexual community has political power from the President to the senators and the representatives. Homosexuality is taught in the schools, the military and it is not a sin in Christianity or the church. The UK long ago passed same-sex marriage legislation and many states in the US have done so as well. As for states that have not, the issue is on the tables of the Supreme Court. With support from the United Nations, white Christian powers, particularly the UK and the USA will force every country in Africa, the Middle East and Asia to have same-sex marriages or sanctions. Lastly, the spread of this disease will never end, because sex is a powerful and enjoyable act. With the promotion of sex on TV, the radio, the internet, and at the workplace, sex is just one of the white powerful government methods to depopulate the world also known as their sustainability act.

All the citizens within the USA that have been killed or injured by a gun after the year 1900 should blame the 2nd amendment. Second, the founding fathers who wrote it, third, Dianne Feinstein and her 99 white senator friends who supports it, fourth, the 435 representatives and lastly, the man who lives at 1600 Pennsylvania avenue, DC, because they will not destroy this amendment. In England or the UK, their citizens cannot buy guns or have guns. There are no gun stores or gun shows and furthermore, the police carry no guns. Most criminal crimes are committed by stabbings using knives. Planned stabbing takes a lot of guts because the perpetrator will look his victim in the eyes and have to come within arm's length to execute the battery. Also, it is difficult to kill more than one victim at a time, as opposed to the nature of a gun (just turn and shoot) that can shoot multiple people at close range. However, the US jurisprudence system makes millions of dollars each year solely because of "the Gun." What's more important making money or saving lives! In capitalism, a greed-based usury society endorses evil behavior because money rules. There were well over 500 murders in Chicago, Illinois in the year 2012, not counting the many other city-states that hold mostly black inner-city people. How many of these funerals will Michelle Obama attend? Attending one funeral and giving one family condolences does not make things better for the next Chicagoan that will be gunned down. Black Chicagoans need to understand that although they have a black president who was first an Illinois senator, efforts were not made on his behalf to improve the situation of Blacks as a senator and the same is true for the president. He does not represent one single Black American.

The Europeans long ago put limits on the many Christian faiths and or put them in check-mate using secularism and science. The bible is a disrespected book there, the church stay closed mostly and on Sunday there are lots of vacant seats. In the US their secularism is presently murdering Muslims all over the world. They also attack the Islamic book the Quran and the Last Prophet, Muhammad. The west wants its people to love, respect and obeys the founding father's bill of rights and therefore disgraces all other religious books. And the people are living these practices therefore they have no morals. The US government, the sorry 100 senators and the lower house don't want to admit the faults of the written constitution. Religiously Moses" people were not shining they never made it to the promised land, surely Jesus was not shining being accused and attacked by the Roman Empire and being betrayed by his own people and today's Muslims are many but not shining and extremely weak in faith. However is the west shining with its individualism, materialism, and weapons of mass destruction, arrogant leadership, everyday violent behaviors and immoral behaviors all supported by the US government? Lastly, at the end of the day, Muhammad (Pbuh)had seen Moses and Jesus in Heaven during his ascension. But today these dominating secularist people all make confession to follow no Prophet, therefore, they are doomed for this decision and to a no-hope future at death and surely we all will die.

The United States is a comical government, reminiscent of Mickey Mouse, Donald Duck and Looney Tunes. If a student takes a course in political science, the first chapter of the textbook will state, "The Government laws or legislations take precedence." Therefore, the state comes second. But practicality begins on the street and the states have the last word and or the enforcement of the laws. A perfect example is a federal government stating that marijuana is illegal but some states allow people to purchase marijuana for medical and recreational purposes. The same with many other issues the federal states the law but the State rules with practicality. The US Constitution, federal statutes and the US legal system mandate that all state judges follow federal laws when a conflict arises between federal laws and the state constitution or state law. Throughout the whole Jim Crow Era, the states used nullification, the legal theory that states have the right to nullify or invalidate federal laws which they viewed as being unconstitutional. So again, the state rules.

To become a lawyer it may take four to six years of college, plus three more years of law school and maybe another year to study for the state bar examination. Furthermore, these lawyers have to practice law for a number of years before becoming a judge. However, the US court system selects people off the street to be, "jurors of their peers." It is considered a civic duty for citizens to determine or "judge" the outcome of a criminal case by stating whether the defendant is guilty or not guilty. These people don't understand the law; even though, the judges may educate the jurors about the laws for about 15 minutes by reading procedure information. However, if the people take a vocabulary test of each other professional terminologies there is a great chance they will all fail respectively. For example, a teacher, a doctor, a mechanic, a finance broker, and most important a lawyer, in each profession further information is needed during and after service. In the criminal courtroom of the US with so many jurisprudences do other professional people understand procedures and what is being said? This system favors the criminal because if there is one juror that is brain dead, a moron, or an imbecile they all will create a hung juror. Also, the system discriminates when it comes to most foreigners, most jurist selections are ten whites and two black, no Chinese, no Africans, no Arabs, no Indians, no South American, no Asians definitely no Mexican.

The most known statement in America is, "We the people." Is that inclusive of all the people in America who are of any and every race and ethnicity but white and European? In this US government and country, "We the people," are the white race, the super-rich capitalist, and white supremacists, and today the two new, "we the people," groups are the homosexual community and illegal Mexicans. All these people have 100% representation. They are the government's priority and are given preferential treatment over the "non-we the people" groups who are mostly black people, Africans, Middle East and Native Americans. American history shows clearly that the white race has always and will always have priorities over the particular non-white races. However the rich will always blame the weak, and now the new wave of blame is focused on the criminally insane who use guns, but should be institutionalized, said the NRA.

All the people in the world that the European powers have touched, conquered, and interact with; these people will never be the same. There are people from the sub-Saharan part of Africa, Christian Africans that love white people more than they love their parents. There are many countries again mostly in the sub-Saharan area and mostly Christian Blacks love that the British and France came; conquered, enslaved and now they can speak one to two European languages, because of the force in changing in culture, customs, social institutions, daily behavior and the most effective acculturation the psychological and physical wellbeing of these people. And the same is true for the black Christian Americans they are conditioned to follow behind white people and worse they follow the evil behavior of these people which caused the black people to look disgusted in society, land in jail and be victims of society. Most of the native people and or indigenous people before the white European Christian invasion lived in a peaceful group, they were no criminals, no capitalism, no individualism, no alcoholics and most important no Christianity. Today from the land down under Australia, the Christian Aboriginals, the Christians of South East Asia, Christians of Indians, South African Christians, native American Christians and the worse Black American Christians have a long history of ethnic crime against their own ethnicity. Also South American countries of Brazil and Colombia have strong histories of violence and these countries are predominate Christian. Again because of three strong ingredients white man's persuasion, secularism, and Christianity all cause the non-white people to open up to more white persuasion resulting in more disgrace and the destruction of their own minds, bodies and souls.

From a fledgling Union of 13 colonies, the United

States has grown to dominate the world power of fifty states spanning the entire continent and beyond. The new constellation of our founding fathers now has received the malevolence baton of the ferocious British Empire, to aggressively conquer, dictate world policies, push their totalitarianism, their regressive and progressive imperialism, to assault and thread, and to spread violence around the globe world. For now, it can truly be said, that these US is the sole superpower of the world, can start wars, have weapons of mass destruction, force their political and economic system on weaker nations, surely no justice for all and torture, sophisticated wars, surveillance and drone murdering attacks of non-Christian people will continue in the future.

Humpty-Dumpty sat on the wall
Humpty-Dumpty had a great fall.
All the King's horses and all
The King's men
Couldn't put Humpty-Dumpty
Together again

The United States of America will eventually fall like Humpty-Dumpty. The United States government, economy and social ethics are falling at this very moment. When the power shatters on the floor, all the 100 white Senators with their legislative pens and all of the soldiers with their weapons of mass destruction will not be able to put the country together again. The end!!!

Bibliography and Reference

The Quran. **Authorized Abdullah Yusuf Ali:**

The Bible. **Authorized King James Version**:
Hadith: **the records and saying of Muhammad**

webspace.ship.edu/cgboer/heresies.html "Early Christian Heresies" Dr. C. George Boeree:
en.wikipedia.org/wiki/Treaty_of_Granada_(1491:

Jameelah, Maryam. *Westernization and Human Welfare.* New Delhi, 1934: 10 (ibid)chapter 6

en.wikipedia.org/wiki/Wounded_Knee_Massacre

Editor L. Frank Baum, later the author of *The Wonderful Wizard of Oz*, wrote in the Aberdeen Saturday Pioneer on January 3, 1891:

en.wikipedia.org/wiki/Gippsland_massacres:
www.sju.edu/~brokes/jimcrow.htm:
en.wikipedia.org/wiki/Civil_and_political_rights:

http://www.hobotraveler.com/colony.php:

www.**frederickdouglass**.org/**douglass** bio.html:

Minority News, Voter Suppression: *The new Jim Crow*, by Willie Brown. MLA Brown, Willie. *Voter Suppression: The new Jim Crow.* Minority News, Oct. 2012.

www.afa.org/media/enolagay/07-93.asp:
Yahoo! News *Jimmy Carter accuses US of widespread abuse of human rights*:
By Amy Bingham/ABC news:
History of Islam Vol. II, Islamic Publications, Lahore (Pakistan)

Lewis, Bernard. *What went wrong*: Oxford University press 2002:

Linda Jacobs Altman. *Slavery and Abolition in American History*: Enslow publishers 1999.

Mary Frances Berry. *Long memory the black experience in America*: New York Oxford University press 1982.

Mark Ray Schmidt, *the 1970's*: Greenhaven press, inc. San Diego 2000.

Tom Burrell, *Brainwashed*: Smileybooks, New York 2010. http://www.infoplease.com/encyclopedia/society/australi an-

www.guardian.co.uk/.../apr/.../imperialism-didnt-end-international-la

www.ingramcontent.com/pod-product-compliance
Lightning Source LLC
Chambersburg PA
CBHW051945090426
42741CB00008B/1274